KT-450-820

of related interest

When Anxiety Attacks
Terian Koscik
ISBN 978 1 84819 284 3
eISBN 978 0 85701 232 6

Stop Panic Attacks in 10 Easy Steps
Using Functional Medicine to Calm Your Mind
and Body with Drug-Free Techniques
Sandra Scheinbaum
ISBN 978 1 84819 246 1
eISBN 978 0 85701 192 3

Can I Tell You About Anxiety?
A Guide for Friends, Family and Professionals
Lucy Willetts and Polly Waite
Illustrated by Kaiyee Tay
ISBN 978 1 84905 527 7
eISBN 978 0 85700 967 8
Part of the Can I tell you about...? series

A Short Introduction to Helping
Young People Manage Anxiety
Carol Fitzpatrick
ISBN 978 1 84905 557 4
eISBN 978 0 85700 989 0

Teen Anxiety
A CBT and ACT Activity Resource Book
for Helping Anxious Adolescents
Raychelle Cassada Lohmann
ISBN 978 1 84905 969 5
eISBN 978 0 85700 859 6

We're all MAD here

The No-Nonsense Guide to Living with Social Anxiety

Claire Eastham
Foreword by Natasha Devon MBE

Jessica Kingsley *Publishers*
London and Philadelphia

Disclaimer: Every effort has been made to ensure that the information contained in this book is correct, but it should not in any way be substituted for medical advice. Readers should always consult a qualified medical practitioner before adopting any complementary or alternative therapies. Neither the author nor the publisher takes responsibility for any consequences of any decision made as a result of the information contained in this book.

First published in 2017
by Jessica Kingsley Publishers
73 Collier Street
London N1 9BE, UK
and
400 Market Street, Suite 400
Philadelphia, PA 19106, USA

www.jkp.com

Copyright © Claire Eastham 2017
Foreword copyright © Natasha Devon 2017

All rights reserved. No part of this publication may be reproduced in any material form (including photocopying, storing in any medium by electronic means or transmitting) without the written permission of the copyright owner except in accordance with the provisions of the law or under terms of a licence issued in the UK by the Copyright Licensing Agency Ltd. www.cla.co.uk or in overseas territories by the relevant reproduction rights organisation, for details see www.ifrro.org. Applications for the copyright owner's written permission to reproduce any part of this publication should be addressed to the publisher.

Warning: The doing of an unauthorised act in relation to a copyright work may result in both a civil claim for damages and criminal prosecution.

Library of Congress Cataloging in Publication Data
Names: Eastham, Claire.
Title: We're all mad here : the no-nonsense guide to living with social
    anxiety / Claire Eastham.
Other titles: No-nonsense guide to living with social anxiety
Description: London ; Philadelphia : Jessica Kingsley Publishers, 2017.
Identifiers: LCCN 2016038896 | ISBN 9781785920820 (alk. paper)
Subjects: LCSH: Social phobia. | Social phobia--Treatment. | Anxiety. |
    Anxiety--Treatment.
Classification: LCC RC552.S62 E27 2017 | DDC 616.85/225--dc23 LC record
available at https://lccn.loc.gov/2016038896

British Library Cataloguing in Publication Data
A CIP catalogue record for this book is available from the British Library

ISBN 978 1 78592 082 0
eISBN 978 1 78450 343 7

Printed and bound in Great Britain

CONTENTS

FOREWORD

When my mental illness was at its most acute, I used to scour bookshelves looking for anything that might help me make sense of what I was going through. What I found was an avalanche of highly triggering, instructional and self-pitying material, which, rather than leaving me feeling hopeful about the prospect of recovery, actually added to my depression and despair.

In desperation, I took to the internet. I stumbled into forums of users essentially competing to see who had the 'worst' mental illness, forming exclusive 'clubs' where tips for the most toxic possible coping mechanisms were shared. I was also subjected to endless contradictory advice on the subject of medication and 'best' therapies and hideous trolling press pieces describing my illness as an imaginary phenomenon, 'attention-seeking' and 'an insult' to people who had 'real' problems, like cancer. (That will teach me to click on the *Daily Mail* website.)

What I wanted, during that time, was a resource I could rely on. I wanted someone who understood how to simultaneously acknowledge the seriousness of my (very real) condition, but who could also reassure me that I was going to be okay. I needed practical advice that would allow me untangle all of the medical jargon and bold promises of 'cures' - advice which was not sponsored by specific therapy providers or pharmaceutical companies, and took into account that there is no magic solution that is guaranteed to work for everyone.

In short, what I really could have done with was this book.

A note about the author: Claire Eastham's personality leaps from the pages of *We're All Mad Here* and gives you an enthusiastic cuddle. If you haven't fallen in love with her by the time you're finished then we probably wouldn't get on.

Claire bounced into my life at a conference during the autumn of 2015 and asked if she could interview me for her blog. Something about her demeanour and way of expressing herself made me smile. I immediately deemed her to be one of life's Ace People and acquiesced to her request.

We met for lunch in South Kensington a few weeks later. Claire's subsequent take on proceedings turns self-deprecation into an art form. In her blog she describes her thought processes as she approached our table ('*Oh my God, you're going to make a fool of yourself*'). She declares that I am '*without a doubt...intimidating*' (an observation that is both alarming and hilarious if you are me. Which I am). She finishes by detailing how she *'clumsily knock[ed] the saltshaker over'* and I *'politely pretend[ed] not to notice'*.

I've never been able to pretend anything (anyone who has seen my resting bitch face when interrogating right-wing journalists on Sky News will attest). I genuinely didn't notice the 'saltshaker incident' (as it shall be referred to, heretofore). I walked away from our lunch merely cherishing the distinct and unmistakable glow one gets when one has just encountered an official Ace Person.

Later, when my husband asked me what I'd been up to that day, I described Claire as 'funny, Northern and not in any way a dick'. This is, I still believe, a pretty good summary. (I consider humour and non-dickishness to be pre-requisites amongst my social acquaintances. Northern-ness is an added bonus. Not everyone, I realise, can be Northern. I myself, for example, am not – and whilst I recognise it as a substantial flaw in my character I try not to beat myself up too much about it.)

It was the voice of the acute social anxiety Claire has lived with since adolescence that was echoing through her mind on the day of the saltshaker incident. Yet I, the casual observer, would never have known. Anxiety, whilst hideously all-consuming when you're engulfed in it, can be impossible to spot from the outside. Anyone you know could be experiencing it, no matter how

self-assured or confident they might appear. I find
that notion both distressing and strangely comforting.

Whilst we might all be mad here, we are definitely
not alone.

Natasha Devon MBE
September 2016

ACKNOWLEDGEMENTS

This book is dedicated to everyone who lives with social anxiety. You're not a freak, a loser or, most importantly, alone.

Thank you to my editor, Rachel Menzies, and the team at Jessica Kingsley Publishers.

Thank you to my family for their endless support, my closest friends who will happily flash their boobs if I'm having a panic attack and, finally, thank you to my rock and the love of my life Dan.

Introduction

SOCIAL ANXIETY AND ME

Come on, you can do this. Just keep it together. You've been practising all night, you'll be fine. Why haven't they arrived yet? This room is too small. Oh God, it's happening again. Heart is racing and chest is tight. Why can't I move my arms properly? I won't be able to speak, I'll faint. I'm going to make a fool of myself. I have to get out of here now.

This is the day I walked out of an interview for a job that I really wanted, minutes before it began. I had (what I now know to be) a panic attack – the worst of my life.

I say 'walked', but it was more of a frantic run. I screamed in the confused HR woman's face that I had the 'norovirus and need to leave at once!' Not a bad off-the-cuff excuse, considering my brain was in pieces. Also, I don't think I've ever used the phrase 'at once' before...or since. I seem to morph into Jane Austen mode when in dramatic situations!

Was the incident a shock? No. I knew before I went in that something bad was going to happen. I'd known when I got up in the morning, when I was travelling to work and when I drank my coffee. The dread was there and I knew, but I just didn't want to believe it. I couldn't.

The next two weeks were a blur, filled with hysteria, emotional outbursts and constant panic, which made it impossible to think rationally. What was happening to me?

✖   ✖   ✖

The term 'anxiety' was first batted about when I was 14, although personally I think I've had it from an early age. As a child I dreaded big family gatherings. My favourite thing to do was hang out with my grandma in the kitchen. She'd drink wine, chain smoke endless amounts of cigarettes and tell me stories. To be honest, not much has changed in that area, the only difference being that I can now join her in the drinking!

I struggled at secondary school and blushed violently whenever anyone spoke to me. I avoided most interactions and constantly worried about being asked a question in class. Think of me as a smoke alarm, primed to go off at the slightest indication of danger.

In English lessons we read *Macbeth* together as a class and everyone was expected to read a scene aloud. A nice inclusive activity, right? Wrong. It was my personal idea of torture! I knew when my turn was coming up because it was all done in alphabetical order. So for the first half of the lesson I didn't listen to a word that was said, because I was too busy freaking out. Despite being completely literate, as soon as it was my turn to read, I couldn't speak properly. The silence of the room was deafening as I stumbled over the words as fast as I could. It was agonising and I was convinced that everyone was laughing at me. To this day I have no idea what happened in *Macbeth*!

Another fond memory was doing role play exercises with the teacher in French class. A student would be randomly selected to come to the front and 'show off' their French conversation skills. Why do teachers always think this type of thing is fun? It's not fun! Most teens find it awkward at best and excrutiating at worst. The not knowing if I'd be chosen was the hardest part for me. I would hold my breath and physically brace myself as the teacher scanned the room. Thoughts like 'I'll die if she chooses me' played on loop in my head. The one time that I was chosen, I could barely say my name I was freaking out so bad, aware that all eyes were on me and my trembling voice. Why couldn't I just get on with it like the other kids?

Around this time, it became clear to me that I was developing some emotional issues. So I did what every 'sensible' adolescent would do: I ignored them (because ignoring a problem always works, right?). I thought this was the best way to deal with my issues – that is, by refusing to let them control my life. As hard as it was, I didn't let them stop me making friends, passing my exams, getting into university, achieving my degree and getting a job. They were something I simply endured. (During my university years I thought that alcohol helped a lot, but more about that later.)

When it came to choosing a career, I soon realised that owning a corner shop wasn't as much fun as the game I played with my brother when we were kids. My love of books drew me to the publishing industry and I was prepared to work really hard to achieve this dream. To be frank, it's not easy for a working-class, non-London-based girl to get a job in publishing, or in the media for that matter. Experience is required and when you live 300 miles away, it isn't easily obtained. So I did a Master's degree in Publishing and then I accepted a month-long internship at a well-known publishing house. It was strange to be away from home for so long, but I was excited about the opportunity. During the internship I stayed in a hostel frequented by drug-taking backpackers and very confident naked German women. (Would it be too much to ask to cover up at 7am? Apparently so.) It was a cold and grotty place, but I couldn't afford a hotel. Let's just say I cried a lot during those weeks! Nevertheless, the internship was a really positive experience and made the living arrangements worthwhile. I enjoyed the work and the atmosphere was passionate and electric. It confirmed to me that publishing was the industry I wanted to be in.

I was therefore overwhelmed with joy when I was offered a full-time job at the same publishing house a few months later. I moved from my home town of Bolton to London on a sunny day in March. Did I know anybody there? No. Had I spent much time in London previously? Not really. Was I comfortable moving away from the safety of the nest to share a house with two complete strangers for £680 a month? F**k no. Don't even get me started on London prices. Seriously, don't. 'Shell shock' doesn't even begin to describe it.

At the time, people would tell me how brave and fearless I was, but I didn't really consider this. Why? Simple: I was in complete denial about the enormous thing I was doing. It was too much to process, so I simply jumped right in at the deep end and swam wildly.

It all started out well enough. The housemates were nice, I worked out how to use the underground (eventually), and I had a Starbucks coffee on my way to work every day, just like in the films. (For a smalltown girl this was the coolest thing ever.) I even found myself a boyfriend six weeks after my arrival – someone who didn't know anything about my past (and I intended to keep it that way).

I was officially living the dream! All those bad times were behind me and I was a new person now... Right?

Six months after my arrival I started to notice some changes in myself. I felt unhappy, irritable and lethargic four working days out of five. The department I worked in at the time was full of loud and dominant characters, which made me feel uneasy and tense. An extrovert personality seemed vital in order to get noticed, whereas I'm more of an introvert (not to be confused with being shy!). There were so many publicity events that I was expected to attend and, like the family parties, I dreaded each one, but there was no grandma to save me this time. Instead, I was on my own in a sea of bright lights and strange faces.

I slowly became obsessed with what people thought of me and how I presented myself. I didn't want to care, but I couldn't stop myself. I even analysed how I walked down a corridor. It became a phobia. Should I smile at people? Should I look at the floor? What? WHAT?! By the time the person actually walked past me, I was having facial spasms! Lifts were another problem: I couldn't bear the thought of a stilted conversation with a colleague. So I ended up walking seven floors worth of stairs every day. Great for exercise, bad for sweat! The staff kitchen was a minefield, too - you never knew who would be in there. What if I couldn't think of anything to talk about? So again, I steered clear of it. There was just so much to avoid in the world!

Then the physical symptoms started: blushing, rapid heartbeat, breathlessness and insomnia. On occasions, when I actually fell asleep, I would wake up hours later with a start, covered in sweat and gasping for air. Worst of all were the tremors. At one point, my hands would shake so regularly that I was afraid to pass items to my colleagues in case they noticed.

Eventually, in a fit of tears I asked myself if I was even happy any more. Why couldn't I concentrate on anything? What was wrong with me? Why couldn't I just be normal for once in my life?

Did I tell anyone at this point? Of course not. I was the brave girl living the dream! The idea of admitting that I was struggling filled me with shame. It was better to keep on pretending.

Looking back, it's obvious that all those 'niggling' thoughts were setting the stage for the panic attacks that eventually developed. Constantly fighting my anxiety put both my brain and body under immense strain, and ultimately they couldn't cope. After ten years, I had finally pushed myself too far.

After the 'interview incident' or 'Interviewgate', I had what they tell me was a nervous breakdown and I was signed off work for a month. This devastated me at first, as I had always kept my condition private. However, in time I realised that it was the right thing. I needed time to heal.

I'd been fighting and hiding this problem all my life, but now here it was written in plain English on my doctor's note: 'acute social anxiety disorder'. In a way, I was relieved because 'It' finally had a name; but on the other hand, I was terrified because I didn't know what to do. I didn't even know where to start. I was convinced that I was going to lose everything that I had worked so hard to get. Worst of all, I was going to lose my boyfriend, Dan.

So what happened next? Well I'll be honest: it was really, really, really bad for a while. You can't cure ten years' worth of damage in a few days. Ask the Romans - you can't build shit in a day.

However, the most important thing to highlight is, I *did* recover and the girl who could barely hold a conversation without trembling and blushing can now give presentations in front of hundreds of people. Don't get me wrong, it's still not my idea of fun, but I can do it confidently. Unbelievable, right? Sometimes I struggle to believe it myself. But I can assure you that it's all true and at no point did I join a cult.

I dealt with my issues, worked hard and kept going. Was it easy? NO. Did I feel like giving up at times? YES. But I got there.

Here's my first piece of advice and it's *very* important: **YOU NEED TO ACCEPT THAT YOU HAVE A MENTAL CONDITION.** You can't heal if you don't accept it, that's just the way it is. Take ownership of it.

Along the dusty road to recovery I picked up some useful tips and tricks, which I believe *actually work*. I hope to share them with you in this book, along with lots of personal experiences (apologies in advance, but you can always skip through these).

The techniques I recommend are simple and accessible to everyone. I'm not a fan of anything that costs £100 a session, or activities that require chanting. (I tried that once and I felt like a dick.)

I began writing my blog – *We're All Mad Here* – in 2014. It was partly for therapeutic reasons and partly because I wanted to help others realise that anxiety is more common than you think.

For the record, I am neither a doctor nor a psychologist. I'm just a normal girl who has a great deal of experience with feeling anxious and generally freaking out! I hope to share what I've learned, in a genuine and straightforward way. No medical jargon will appear without a simple definition.

Social anxiety is a very treatable condition – one that you don't have to be ashamed of, or deal with alone. I'm right there with you.

I hope that by the time you've finished reading this book, you'll finally be ready to accept who you are and have faith that things can and will get better.

Is there anything else you need to know? Well... I don't write like an academic and I like to swear. A LOT! You've been warned.

'We're all mad here, I am, you are. But I'll
tell you a secret...all the best people are.'

LEWIS CARROLL, ALICE IN WONDERLAND, 1865

Chapter 1

WHAT THE HELL IS IT AND WHY IS IT HAPPENING TO ME?

How can a person recover if they don't understand what they're dealing with? This is a simple question and if the logic applies to physical health, why should mental health be any different?

Identifying the source of any illness removes that element of fear and confusion. The question 'Why do I feel this way?' deserves an answer. If you were experiencing pain in your back, you'd want to know what was causing it, right? Replies such as 'It's all in your head' or 'You just need to try and relax' wouldn't be satisfactory! In order to answer this question in relation to anxiety, I'm going to explain a little more about the human brain and how it works. This is by far the most complex chapter in the book, but if you can soldier through it I promise that you'll be armed with a better understanding of mental health.

When I had my breakdown, I immediately asked myself the following questions:

- ✖ What is social anxiety disorder?

- ✖ Why is it happening to me?

- ✖ How do I make it go away?

I lost count of the hours I spent typing 'social anxiety' into Google, time and again desperately searching for answers. So allow me to clarify...

WHAT IS SOCIAL ANXIETY DISORDER?

Medical definition: A fear or phobia related to social situations.

Claire definition: The idea of social gatherings or being the centre of attention making you feel sick with dread. You're convinced that you're going to make a fool of yourself and everyone present will notice and judge you. No amount of reassurance from loved ones will help – in fact, it often makes things worse.

Common physical symptoms include:

- ✖ blushing – sometimes for no reason at all
- ✖ shaking/tremors
- ✖ sweating
- ✖ nausea
- ✖ a dry mouth
- ✖ tense muscles
- ✖ stuttering or mumbling
- ✖ feeling light-headed
- ✖ a constant need to use the toilet.

As a teenager I would blush crimson whenever someone merely said my name! Picture this scene:

Teacher: Claire, your homework was very good this week.

Me: *Turns the colour of an angry tomato* Thank you.

Teacher: *Looks confused* Are you OK, Claire?

Me: *Turns almost purple* Yes, I'm fine, Miss, I'm just a bit hot. *Thinks, 'Oh my God I'm so embarrassed I could die. Why am I so weird?'*

Before parties or nights out I would pee more times than a puppy in training. I think every five minutes was my record. Once, before an interview (not my favourite environment), I had to use the reception bathroom three times in ten minutes. After my last visit, I approached the desk and said, 'Don't worry, I wasn't doing cocaine and I don't have diahorrea!' The receptionist didn't laugh (people rarely laugh at my jokes); in fact, she probably hadn't even noticed and therefore thought I was a nutter.

Over time I became more nervous about the physical symptoms occurring during a social occasion than about the actual event itself. Talk about irony! For example, 'Oh God I have a meeting today, I know I'm going to start blushing.' This would naturally trigger a blush attack. It's what we call a vicious circle!

Common mental and emotional symptoms include:

- ✖ Negative thoughts, such as 'Everyone will think I'm an idiot/a loser/boring' or 'I'm so ugly, nobody will ever find me attractive.' Personally, I convince myself that other people don't actually want to talk to me – they're just doing it out of pity.

- ✖ An overwhelming fear that you're going to embarrass yourself.

- ✖ Over-analysing past situations to a clinical level. For example, 'James looked at me weird earlier. I don't think he likes me. Maybe I've done something to annoy him?' Alternatively, 'Why the f**k did I say that? They must've thought I was a complete idiot.' You go through every single detail like a private investigator – I once spent half a day replaying a conversation in my head.

✖ An obsession with how you appear physically, rather than feeling comfortable in the moment. You analyse all of your actions and behaviours. I used to do a body scan: Am I sweating? Are my hands shaking? Do I look friendly and relaxed? Am I asking the right questions?

✖ Making extreme negative predictions about future events. For example, 'The party is going to be awful. I'll start sweating and everyone will notice. I'll have to make an excuse and leave, then throw myself under a double-decker bus or through a window.' (See, I said 'extreme'.)

✖ Self-loathing and criticism. Sometimes I actually used to shout at myself in the staff bathroom (alone, obviously). 'You stupid bitch, why can't you behave like a normal person!' That's an encouraging pep talk, right? Maybe a punch in the face to accompany it?

✖ Feeling insecure, ashamed and unhappy.

In a nutshell, social anxiety is being hyper-aware of how you're perceived by others and having an overpowering fear/obsession about looking like an idiot.

WHY IS IT HAPPENING TO ME?

Another classic and natural question is 'Why have I been selected?'

Some people can remember an event that triggered their anxiety – a traumatic incident that left deep scars. Others (like me) have no idea what started it. I was born into a stable and happy home. We weren't rich but we got by just fine. I have a solid group of friends and I'm lucky enough to be physically healthy. So what's the problem? I don't know... How long is a piece of string?

Personally, I think I was just born with an overly active nervous system that heightened as I grew up and was exposed to more of life. I also think it's fair to say that I was always a sensitive child/teenager/ grown woman. A few classic examples spring to mind:

✖ When I found out that Santa Claus wasn't real, I was so distraught that I very dramatically put myself to bed. It was as though a member of the family had died and I howled into my pillow. (I was definitely too old for this level of reaction.) In contrast, my brother worked it out one Christmas Eve when he spied Dad wheeling his new bike around downstairs. He was totally cool with it and went back to sleep.

✖ I had to take the day off school when I found out Stephen Gately (Boyzone) was gay. I was only seven, but I knew he was the man I wanted to marry.

✖ I hid behind a tree for half an hour to avoid a friend's birthday party. Eventually, his mum spotted me. Bitch.

✖ I once slept with a scarf around my neck for three months because I was scared of vampires. Pity it was summer.

✖ *Watership Down* traumatised me for...let's see... the last 15 years! Bunnies aren't supposed to behave like that. Why are they so freaking angry?

But I digress. My point is that I don't waste time trying to pinpoint an exact moment when my anxiety started. Studies suggest that, like many illnesses, an anxious condition is hereditary. In my opinion though, there's no point pinning the blame on members of your family. It won't solve anything.

The evolution of the brain

To explain the development of anxiety as a whole, I need to strip things back to basics. (Basics as in the dawn of mankind and how the brain evolved!) Let's use the traditional example and imagine a caveman, complete with a nice loincloth, shaggy hair and one of those clubs from the cartoons. Do we think that our caveman spent his nights worrying about what the other cavemen thought of him? Before he went to sleep, did he think, 'Oh God, I hope I don't bump into Dave at the water hole tomorrow – I never know what to say. I'll bet he thinks I'm so boring'? I'm no historian, but I doubt it. He was probably more concerned with sabre-toothed tigers, finding food and creating fire.

So what happened? Why has this simplistic way of being changed so much? Well, according to American physician and neuroscientist Paul MacLean (1990), humans have three brains (all with typically complicated names):

✖ mammalian/frontal lobe (basically, the emotional part, or the subconscious)

✖ lizard (the stem/main battery for the physical body)

✖ cortex/human (the rational and thinking part).

MacLean believes that these brains grew on top of each other, with the cortex being the youngest and therefore the weakest. We humans like to think that we can control our emotions – 'mind over matter', yes? But in reality the mammalian is the strongest part of the brain. (Shit!) This is fine in theory, except that our older and emotional brain is concerned with core basic things:

✖ love (humans are social creatures, we crave the affection and acceptance of others)

✖ sex (procreation)

✖ danger (we don't want to die or suffer injury).

When any of the above are strongly present in a situation, then the emotional brain takes over and the rational brain doesn't stand a chance.

Think about it: have you ever texted an ex-partner when you *know full well* that it's a bad idea? Even as you're typing you know it's a mistake, but you can't stop. Or have you obsessed about a dispute with a colleague when it isn't actually a big deal? Surely you should just let it go? But you can't because she spoke over you in that meeting and made you look like an idiot. BITCH! (Clearly I'm not over that one just yet.)

My point is this: we criticise ourselves for being weak-minded. I used to say things like 'I'm not mentally strong' or ask 'Why can't I just be normal?' However, in reality my emotional brain was in the driving seat, so beating myself up was counter-productive. Would you shout at yourself because you had a broken arm? For example, 'Oh my God you're such a loser. I can't believe that fall down the stairs broke your arm. You should be ashamed!' or 'I can't believe you have a headache, that's so embarrassing. You should just crawl under your bed and never come out.' Of course you bloody wouldn't, because it's not your fault!

Humans are driven by emotions, *not* logic or common sense. The automatic physical reactions triggered by said emotions were, and still are, our greatest survival techniques. You'll probably have heard about the 'fight or flight' complex? Well the commander of this automatic response is called the amygdala. (Personally I would've called it 'the smoke alarm' or 'spider sense', but someone clearly thought that amygdala was the better choice.) Have you ever nearly fallen down some stairs, but at the last second your arm moved at rapid speed and grabbed a rail? You didn't think about it – it just happened. That was your amygdala doing its job. Its sole purpose is to keep you alive. How does it do that? Well, it recognises potentially dangerous situations and floods the body with extra adrenalin (energy) to increase reaction times and strength. Adrenalin is the body's natural super serum. (For the record, my amygdala is shit hot. Sometimes I jump when a door closes. Seriously, I'd be awesome in an apocalyptic-type situation!)

From a caveman's perspective, this state of affairs was great. Everything was very simple then: avoid danger, find a partner and join other cavemen. During this period, being negative helped humans to survive – if the brain is not sure about a situation, it will automatically assume the worst and go into self-preservation mode. It also has an excellent memory database. For example, 'We were attacked by a lion previously, so I'm going to put lions on the danger list.' Sounds great, right?

Unfortunately, aggressive managers have replaced sabre-toothed tigers and the venue for making friends has switched from the camp fire to school or the workplace, in which often only the coolest people survive. The process has become over-complicated. The world changed faster than our brain could evolve and the emotional brain isn't equipped to deal with it. The amygdala can't find a suitable response. Think about it: you can't run out of a meeting or hit your boss over the head with a club.

Police officer: Tell me again why you smashed your manager in the face with a baseball bat?

Me: Because he asked me to talk in a meeting.

Perhaps you had a bad experience once at a party and felt embarrassed. The amazing amygdala may therefore decide to put 'parties' on the danger list, along with lions. It's an automatic reaction. Why does this happen to you? You simply have a very strong mammalian brain and that's not your fault. If you can accept this principle and be more patient with yourself, you'll have a solid base to begin your recovery.

Brain chemicals

If you've already been to a doctor about your anxiety, you may have heard the terms 'serotonin', 'selective serotonin reuptake inhibitors (SSRIs)' and 'cortisol'. Picture the following scene:

Doctor: You don't have enough serotonin in your body.

Me: Oh my God, what's that? It sounds awful! Am I going to die?

Doctor: No. Serotonin is a compound present in blood platelets and serum. It constricts the blood vessels and acts as a neuro-transmitter.

Me: What's a freaking neurotransmitter?

Doctor: A chemical substance that is released at
               the end of a nerve fibre by the arrival of a
               nerve impulse and, by diffusing across the
               synapse or junction, affects the transfer
               of the impulse to another nerve fibre, a
               muscle fibre, or some other structure.

Me: Tell me...are you taking the piss, or are
               you a robot? (I didn't say that out loud,
               but I thought it really hard.)

It took me weeks and a LOT of internet research to
clarify exactly what she was talking about. To simplify
things I'm going to use the following definitions:

✖ *Serotonin:* This is the calm/happy hormone.
  When doctors use the term 'neurotransmitter',
  they mean a DHL courier that carries signals
  from the nerves to the brain. It is a vital chemical
  that helps the brain to function and keep moods
  and emotions stable. Basically, it's a happy
  messenger that balances out stress levels in the
  brain. That's all you need to know.

✖ *Cortisol:* This is the stress hormone. It's linked
  to adrenalin and helps humans to react quickly
  to potentially dangerous situations. However, it
  can also be released accidentally by the amygdala
  in non-threatening situations. If you're running

late and you feel 'buzzed' and 'jittery', that's most likely the effects of cortisol.

I've heard many analogies in reference to serotonin, but my favourite is a comparison to fuel or diesel. If a car is running low on fuel, it will backfire, jerk and struggle to make the journey. Similarly, if the brain is running low on serotonin, it will still function in a basic sense, but it won't be an easy ride and things will feel that bit harder.

Everybody has a tank full of serotonin, but some people have bigger tanks than others and some burn through their supply faster. It's important to keep the fuel topped up so that the brain can function. It's like keeping your diesel tank topped up to prevent your car from getting stuck in a muddy field, surrounded by cows and one very angry bull! (That really happened to me. My dad was not impressed that he had to drive for three hours to pick me up.)

A lack of serotonin can have a serious impact on the nervous system. It causes the brain to malfunction and freak out. (A freak-out = an anxiety or panic attack.) Try to think of it as the body's natural tranquilliser. If you have anxiety, it's more likely that your levels are depleted. How can you keep them topped up? Keep reading...Chapter 2 has the answers!

Chapter 2

HOW DO I MAKE IT GO AWAY?

I wasted years of my life asking this question. Nobody likes to feel ill. Can you imagine having the flu for ten years? We instinctively look for cures, answers and solutions.

What I'm about to say is not what you'll want to hear, but it's important. **YOU CANNOT MAGICALLY FORCE YOUR ANXIETY TO GO AWAY.** You might as well wish that your left ear would fall off! It is a part of YOU and therefore it isn't going anywhere. However, before you fall into a pit of deep despair, let me tell you the good news. You CAN work with it and there are things that you can do. Social anxiety may always be a part of your personality, but it doesn't have to control your life or make you feel unhappy. There are treatments, along with lots of tips and techniques that can help.

Here are a few things I need you to take on board before we move forward:

- ✖ There is NOTHING to be ashamed of. I spent years of my life feeling embarrassed by my anxiety and punishing myself for 'being weak'. But the truth is it has nothing to do with your strength of character. It's a genuine condition.

- ✖ Social anxiety is much more common that you think and ranges from mild to acute.

- ✖ It won't get better overnight; you have to be prepared to work hard and stick to routines.

- ✖ Beware of following the routine for a few days, then lapsing back into watching TV and pissing about on the internet!

- ✖ Although it may be tempting to look for information and support online, be wary of online forums (see below).

Online forums

A quick side note on online forums – **DON'T DO IT TO YOURSELF**. When I was first diagnosed, I was hungry for information and a connection to others. There's nothing scarier than feeling alone (apart from worrying that someone might be hiding in the wardrobe, but you don't have the balls to go and check).

In an emotional moment I made the mistake of looking at online forums. Dear God, that was a bad idea! I may as well have typed 'I'd like to feel even more depressed about my life' into Google. Forums can be incredibly useful for many things (e.g. restaurant reviews and the best way to get grease out of a shirt) but NOT for mental health advice. Others might disagree with this, but it's an opinion that I'm unlikely to change.

So what's my beef? The lack of context and clean-up. Of course, freedom of speech is a good thing, but it can also be damaging, particularly to a fragile individual who already thinks that her life is over!

Here's a prime example:

> I started having panic attacks three years ago. I quit my job and my girlfriend left me. I never leave the house and I have no friends. Panic attacks have ruined my life and sometimes I wish I could die.
>
> Bob, aged 32

Now, as much as I respect Bob's right to talk about his troubles, I feel like they would've been better directed at a doctor, a mental health professional or a charity. Anxiety UK and Mind both have helplines. Instead, this statement was left in cyber space for me to read and feel even more hopeless about my condition.

> Looking back at Bob's post today, I noticed it was actually written 18 months before I even read it, so it was already out of date. Who knows what happened to Bob? He might have got the help he needed and now be living a happy life. But his words of misery will forever remain on the forum, waiting for other sufferers to read. My point is this: forums can be incredibly damaging to others. They're rarely encouraging, but instead are packed with tales of broken dreams and a reliance on strong medications. Some even appear competitive – for example, 'You think your life is bad? Well listen to this!'

THE CHEMICAL PART

MEDICATION

For want of a better phrase, let's start with the drugs talk! Medication tends to divide people's opinion. Some people are happy to take them, others can't stand the idea. I think it's the zombie image of patients walking around hospital wards in white gowns, with wide eyes and open mouths that people fear (I can't say that I've ever experienced this). The most important thing is to do what is right for you.

I have a very open attitude with regard to prescription medication. I certainly take it seriously, but I also recognise that there's a lot of stigma attached, which I can never quite understand. People take painkillers and antibiotics all the time, so why are 'brain tablets' so much more shameful?

First things first: make an appointment with your doctor. He or she can offer advice and, more importantly, write prescriptions! Sometimes I joke that my doctor is like my 'dealer'. (She never laughs.)

Here, I'm going to discuss each group in detail and without restraint.

Long-term medication
Selective serotonin reuptake inhibitors (SSRIs)

Where do you even begin with a ridiculous name like that? Sometimes I wonder whether the medical industry use OTT jargon just to intimidate (but I'll save that rant for another day).

SSRIs boost the production of serotonin in the brain and are prescribed for a variety of anxiety- and depression-related conditions. I could elaborate, but that's all you really need to know! Remember what I said in Chapter 1 about keeping your fuel tank topped up? Well SSRIs provide a way to do that.

There are a variety of SSRIs available in the UK. According to the NHS, the most common are:

- ✖ citalopram
- ✖ fluoxetine

✖ paroxetine

✖ sertraline.

From personal experience, citalopram and sertraline seem to be the 'go to' ones. These are prescribed for an indefinite period. Initially, you should have a review with your doctor every month, but over time the reviews become less frequent. I have been taking setraline for two years and I now have a check-up with my doctor every six months. Always be sure to attend these appointments. It's an opportunity to voice any concerns that you have and for your doctor to assess whether the medication is improving your condition.

One of the questions/concerns I hear the most is: 'I'm worried about the side effects. What if get addicted? My body should be able to deal with this naturally.'

This strikes a chord. I, too, would like my body to produce more serotonin without me having to take medication. But then I'd also like it to get rid of a migraine, heal a broken arm or indeed shoot bolts of lightning out of my eyes naturally. Sadly, some people need a little medicinal help to control anxiety, so try and look at anxiety medication in the same way that you view treatments for physical conditions.

Are there potential side effects? Of course there are – life is never without its curveballs. But let's put this into context, as the phrase 'side effects' conjures up images of nuclear chemicals and mutant powers. Side effects often occur when you first start taking a medication and the body is trying to acclimatise to the sudden change in chemicals. Most people (including myself) only experience side effects for a few days, whereas some don't get them at all. The most common side effects of SSRIs include:

✖ increased feelings of anxiety (this is your brain freaking out about the new chemical)

✖ feeling sluggish and overtired

✖ nausea

✖ dizziness

✖ blurred vision

✖ low sex drive.

I personally felt very emotional and lethargic at the start of treatment. In other words, I was crying and sleeping for two days. It wasn't pleasant, but it also wasn't something that I couldn't cope with. Is it a pain in the arse? YES. Is it worth it in the end? In my opinion, YES.

> **TIP:** Don't be disheartened if the first medication that you try doesn't work for you. As with many things in life, it's all about trial and error. The right one is out there (just like the truth).

In very rare cases some SSRIs have been known to make a person feel suicidal or deeply depressed. If this happens, consult your doctor *immediately* as this is a sign that the medication doesn't agree with your body. Again it can be sorted, but you *must* seek medical advice.

With regard to addiction, while I wouldn't recommend that you suddenly stop taking any medications (it's better to wean yourself off slowly), SSRIs are not addictive in the 'heroin-addict-lying-on-newspaper-in-squat' kind of way that everybody seems to fear.

Please note that it can often take up to two weeks before you notice any benefits, so don't expect results overnight. Also, remember that SSRIs won't magically cure everything; however, they will make your anxiety more manageable.

Short-term medications

Propranolol – beta blocker

This medication is prescribed if a person suffers mainly from physical symptoms. It can work wonders with problems such as a pounding heart, tremors, sweating and blushing.

Propranolol has actually become the drug of choice for celebrities/high-power business people over the years. I like to call these tablets 'chill pills'. Why? Because they slow the heart rate down (in a safe way – don't freak out!). A doctor once told me that they allow you to be 'yourself at your best', which is why so many people in high-power positions have been known to take one before an important meeting.

However, they won't do *anything* for emotional or mental issues, so don't be tempted to use them as a crutch - the feeling of anxiety will still be present.

I personally only take beta blockers when absolutely necessary - for example, if my tremors are particularly bad or I'm going through a period of stress and my body is struggling.

If physical symptoms are the most distressing for you, then beta blockers might be something to consider. However, again be sure to discuss your options with a doctor.

Zopiclone - sleeping tablet

OK, this one is slightly more hardcore, but it's important to have an honest discussion.

One of my biggest anxiety triggers is a lack of sleep. It makes sense: nobody can function properly if they're tired, whether they have anxiety or not! I've always been a troubled sleeper, and when I'm really stressed this intensifies.

A vicious cycle emerges whereby I can't sleep, so I feel anxious and raw the following day; I then worry that I won't be able to sleep that night; this results in high levels of stress before bedtime, making it impossible to sleep!

After discussing the problem at length with my doctor, it was decided that I should try a short course of zopiclone. It helped to get me back into a regular sleeping pattern again.

✖ Zopiclone is safe and effective for treating sleep problems. If you're struggling to sleep, then for God's sake take one! Don't mess about worrying that 'it's not natural' and all that shit. Sometimes, we need a little help.

✖ Bit obvious – don't drink alcohol when taking it.

✖ Again obvious – only take the recommended dose.

✖ In contrast to SSRIs, zopiclone can cause dependency and shouldn't be taken for more than two weeks straight (but to be honest, after a few days you should be back in a regular pattern anyway).

TIPS: Here are some other tricks that can help if you have trouble sleeping. I would recommend trying these first before requesting medication.

✖ *Nytol:* Try this over-the-counter remedy if you're a bit wary about prescription medicine. It can be quite effective.

✖ *Heat:* Ideally, have a bath. Warm water eases muscular tension. A bath is like a big warm hug.

✖ *Lavender essential oil:* This is a recognised aromatherapy scent to promote relaxation.

Rub a little on your pyjamas or bed sheets (or add a few drops to your bath water).

✖ *Peppermint tea:* This is really good if stomach pain is keeping you awake. I don't normally plug herbal teas, but this one actually works.

✖ *Tensing and releasing:* Deliberately tense various muscles in the body for a good five seconds and then release. This provides a nice wave of comfort.

✖ *Massage:* You can do this yourself –and there's no need for any fancy oils! Spend a few minutes giving your neck and lower back muscles a firm massage to ease any tension.

✖ *Leave your phone, tablet or whatever in another room:* Watching YouTube videos or browsing the internet will not help you sleep.

✖ *Routine:* When I'm having trouble sleeping, I try to stick to a routine as the body responds well to this. For example, get up at 7am and go to bed at 11pm (even if it's the weekend).

Diazepam – tranquilliser

Ahhh, diazepam – Valium, the famous 'wonder drug', also known as 'mother's little helper'. Again, this is more hardcore, but if used *sensibly* it can be very useful and safe. It has benefits as well as potential risks that you need to be aware of:

✖ It's a tranquillising muscle-relaxant and highly effective at relieving the symptoms of anxiety and panic.

✖ It is often called the 'wonder drug' because it combats the physical, mental and emotional symptoms of stress and anxiety. In a nutshell, it's a super sedative!

✖ Naturally there's a catch. No, you don't have to give up your firstborn, but this is NOT a medication that should be taken long term. Overuse can cause dependency. You certainly don't want to get to the stage where you 'need' a hit to feel normal.

✖ Speak to your doctor about dosage – it is generally recommended that diazepam should not be taken for more than two weeks at a time.

✖ Don't get me wrong, my words are certainly not intended to frighten you. Veteran readers of my blog will know that I'm very pro diazepam when needed. As with many things, it all comes down to common sense. If you've been having panic attacks back to back all evening, or your muscles are aching from hours of tension, then it is right to take one. This is exactly what it's for. Why suffer needlessly?

✖ This medication is recommended for sufferers with more extreme symptoms.

✖ As always, please read the instructions carefully. Remember: no drinking, driving or operating heavy machinery with diazepam in your system!

How to manage potential short-term side effects

Here are my dos and don'ts:

✖ DO talk to those closest to you and explain that you might experience side effects. Tell them that you might need their patience and support for a few days.

✖ DO create your own medication plan. For example, if you work Monday to Friday, my advice is to start taking your medication on a Friday. This will give you the weekend to rest and not worry about work. I would also book the Monday off, just to be sure.

✖ DO make sure you have a stock of supplies to get you through the weekend. I'm talking soft tissues, comfy pyjamas, takeaway menus and other nice things such as chocolate, crisps and an endless supply of films/TV programmes to watch. I pretty much got through two box sets in 48 hours!

✖ DO ask questions. Your doctor is there to help, so talk about any concerns that you might have. Book a double appointment if necessary.

✖ DON'T go cold turkey and stop taking your medication before the recommended date because 'you feel better'. This is one of the worst things you can do – it will mess with your hormones and serotonin levels and you will end up feeling much worse. If the time comes when you would like to stop taking medication, then discuss a plan with your doctor.

✖ DON'T buy medication off the internet. Always consult your doctor.

✖ DON'T be embarrassed. There is nothing to be ashamed of (easier said than done, I know). Taking medication for anxiety doesn't make you a freak or a lunatic! If anything, it's a really brave and positive step, plus nobody even needs to know.

NATURAL SUPPLEMENTS

Although in my opinion vitamins and natural supplements are no match for the effects of prescription medication, I do believe that they have strong benefits and I take them daily. If you're wary about taking medication, then the following might be good for starters:

✖ *Omega 3 capsules (fish oil):* These have been proven to increase serotonin levels in the brain. Don't mess about – invest in a decent brand to make sure that the oil is pure. I take three capsules a day, but the dosage can vary depending on the brand so read the instructions on the package carefully. They're bloody big things and need to be taken with loads of water!

✖ *Vitamin B complex:* This helps to support the nervous system. It's also good for energy levels and vitality. Beware – these vitamins will turn your urine bright neon yellow! When I first started taking them I thought I'd become radioactive!

AROMATHERAPY

Never underestimate the power of scent – it's one of our most primitive senses. A strong smell is like an attack on deep centres of the brain. Essential oils have been used for thousands of years for their exquisite aromas and natural healing powers. While I'm not sold on the healing thing, as I doubt a whiff of sage can cure pneumonia, I do believe that scent can trigger emotional reactions. For example, you're stuck on the train and the person next to you has really bad BO. It turns your stomach, right? You feel distressed and irritated. Or when you catch a whiff of something and it takes you back to another time and place. In my case, whenever I smell Chanel No. 5, I'm instantly transported to when I was eight years old and pottering about in my gran's house. It makes me feel happy and safe.

A comforting scent can therefore have positive effects on the mind and body. If you condition your brain to associate a certain smell with feeling calm or relaxed, then you've created a very powerful technique. Aromatherapy is an excellent way to do this. I'm not suggesting that it will stop a panic attack in its tracks, but it does have its benefits.

The following are the best scents for relaxation:

- ✖ *Lavender:* A classic. Very heavy and intoxicating.

- ✖ *Frankincense:* Earthy and comforting. Besides, if it's good enough for Jesus...

- ✖ *Rose:* Many people call this the 'Queen of Stress Relief'.

- ✖ *Ylang ylang:* Popular in spas, and perfect for a bath.

✖ *Geranium:* Uplifting. Sprinkle on a few drops when you take your morning shower.

I tend to rub a little lavender on my pillow and pyjama top at bedtime as I now associate this scent with sleep. I put ylang ylang in the bath as a treat and I burn frankincense during the dark January evenings when I need the aromatherapy equivalent of a hug!

EXERCISE

Exercise naturally burns off adrenalin, balances the mood and increases energy levels. I bang on about exercise a lot in my blog, because I believe it plays an important role in recovery. Believe me, I never thought that I would become a 'gym person' and you certainly won't find me running a marathon any time soon. But exercise really does help, pure and simple.

People with anxiety produce more adrenalin and cortisol than others and it courses through the veins with no means of escape. It's important to find a natural way to release it and rebalance the hormone levels. Exercise is good for everyone. It's a really healthy and natural way to boost the mood.

Obviously, please talk to your doctor before embarking on a new exercise regime (I have to say that for safety reasons). Also, please drink water! Oh, and if you are slim and tend to lose weight easily, remember to eat more food. I accidently lost half a stone when I started running, because I wasn't taking in enough calories. What better excuse to treat yourself to a blueberry muffin after a workout!

There are so many options for exercise these days. If you hate the gym, you could try swimming, team sports, jogging or even an exercise video in your living room (I can't do this because we live in a flat and the one time I tried, the neighbours complained about the baby elephant crashing about upstairs!). Just do anything that gets your heart thumping. I try to do three 30-minute sessions a week.

Another positive aspect of exercise is that it helps your brain get used to having a pounding heart and shortness of breath. This is especially useful for people who suffer from panic attacks. During an attack your brain will convince you that your pounding heart and troubled breathing are extremely dangerous and are a sign of something awful. However, both symptoms can be perfectly normal during the right circumstances, and exercise is one of these. Therefore, if you can acclimatise your brain to both, you'll find it easier to rationalise these symptoms when you're having an attack. A pounding heart and shortness of breath are just reactions to adrenalin.

FOOD

I've never been into dieting, but I do believe in healthy eating. Ironically, when I was first diagnosed with anxiety, the last thing I wanted was a lecture about the benefits of fruit, veg and a healthy lifestyle. 'GIVE ME THE F**KING DRUUUUUUUUUUGS!' I dismissed the idea as nonsense. But these days I've come to recognise the benefits.

To be clear, I don't mean eating nothing but salads and rice cakes: I don't think there's anything more depressing than that. However, there are certain foods that can really help your brain and nervous system.

- ✖ *Salmon:* This is full of Omega 3 oil, which helps the brain to produce serotonin.

- ✖ *Spinach:* This is packed with magnesium, which helps regulate cortisol levels in the body.

- ✖ *Avocado:* This is full of vitamin B, which supports the nervous system. I love it on toast with poached eggs and a sprinkle of black pepper. Yum!

- ✖ *Almonds:* These contain zinc, which is a key nutrient for maintaining a balanced mood. Let's be honest, they're not the tastiest nut out there, but a handful now and again is easy enough to manage. Plus, you can just carry a pack around in your bag.

✖ *Blueberries:* These are classed as a superfood. They are filled with antioxidants and vitamin C, which helps with cell repair (handy if cortisol is battering the hell out of them!).

✖ *Chia seeds:* These are great for energy (good if you're cutting down on coffee).

> **TIP:** I tend to make a smoothie each morning with blueberries, spinach, an apple (for sweetness), goji berries and chia seeds. That way you can bang everything you need in the smoothie maker and you're done for the day. It's the lazy person's dream!

I'm not suggesting that you only eat the above items and nothing else. If somebody tried to take pizza or cheese away from me, I'd wrestle them to the floor! However, just incorporating a few of these foods into your diet can really make a difference.

One of my favourite and really simple brain food recipes is a salmon stir-fry. I'm not a chef, so please be kind.

SALMON STIR-FRY

Serves 1

Ingredients

1 salmon fillet

1 tablespoon of sesame seed oil

1 packet of stir-fry vegetables

1 decent handful of spinach

1 handful of prawns (cooked and peeled)

1 egg

1 packet of brown microwavable rice (yes, microwavable – I'm a lazy cow)

1 tablespoon of soy sauce (add more to taste)

2 teaspoons of chia seeds

Method

Poach the salmon in the oven (check the cooking instructions on the packet).

Heat the oil in a frying pan or wok for around 60 seconds.

Add the stir-fry veg and spinach.

While this is cooking, stick the rice in the microwave.

Break up the salmon into pieces and add to the frying pan with the prawns.

Add the egg and stir like crazy because it will cook fast!

Add the cooked rice.

Add the soy sauce, to taste.

Add the chia seeds. *Et voilà*, you're done!

The following are things to avoid if you're feeling anxious or under stress:

✖ Caffeine – fairly obvious these days, but we all fall for it. (I will expand on my experiences in Chapter 3.) Caffeine increases the production of adrenalin in the body, which is a bad thing. To be clear, I mean any of the following:

 ✖ coffee

 ✖ tea (yep, I'm afraid so)

 ✖ energy drinks – Red Bull might give you wings but it'll also give you the shakes!

✖ Fizzy drinks.

✖ Diet fizzy drinks – diet versions contain aspartame, which depletes serotonin, so these are actually worse for you than drinks containing sugar.

✖ Alcohol – especially the night before a stressful situation. (More on this in Chapter 3.)

MARIJUANA

Marijuana provokes intense debate in the mental health community. Does it improve symptoms or does it make them worse?

Many states across the US have legalised it for medical use, and in India it's been used for over 400 years to treat anxiety, stress and depression. Despite being illegal in the UK, we all know that people still use it. Failing that, they just travel to the Netherlands and use it there!

I'll be honest and say that I'm *not* a fan. Why?

- ✘ It seriously stinks.

- ✘ It can burn the lungs if you do it wrong.

- ✘ The after-effects are highly unpredictable. I actually felt more anxious a few hours after I smoked it. In particular, it increased my palpitations and restlessness. (If the police are reading this, I have totally never smoked marijuana...especially not to seem cool at a party.)

- ✘ It can induce paranoia. I once spent a good hour at a party talking to a boy who was convinced that something bad was going to happen before midnight. He said he could feel it. Then he ate two packets of chocolate biscuits.

Still, many users argue that on the whole marijuana is less harmful than alcohol. It's not a debate that I can comment on to any extent. I just know that it doesn't work for me and there are other more healthy options to try.

THE TALKING PART

I'll never forget my first session with a therapist – it was a circus. First of all, I didn't want to sit down. Then I refused to take my coat off and sat very stiffly on the edge of the chair. When she asked how I was feeling, I kept repeating, 'Fine, yeah, no worries. How are you?' Like I was paying her to have a chat about the weather!

It was excruciating, simply because I wasn't used to talking about my condition so openly. I was convinced that at any moment she would turn on me: 'You're a nutter! I'm calling the white van immediately.' However, after a while I began to relax and understood that my therapist was there to help, not 'catch me out'! Talking to someone impartial in a safe and non-judgemental environment was a godsend. Finally I could discuss in length all the things that had been troubling me for so long, without fear of upsetting anyone or feeling exposed. It felt liberating.

During the first session you can expect the following:

✖ The therapist will introduce themselves and the techniques they use, and outline the structure that each meeting will take.

✖ You will be asked a series of general questions about your condition. For example, 'How many days out of seven do you feel anxious?'

✖ Some questions might be upsetting, such as: 'Do you ever feel like hurting yourself?' Be sure to answer honestly as there is no judgement. The therapist is just trying to assess the level of your condition.

✖ Most people (including me) become very emotional, so bring tissues! There's no shame in it. Discussing things that you don't like to admit (even to yourself) can be upsetting. However, this is also very cathartic. Releasing pent-up emotion and pressure is a good thing. So have a good cry if you need to and don't apologise!

✖ In order to get the most out of your session it's important to be honest. Remember, the therapist is there to support you. There is nothing to be ashamed of and no need to hide. They might even spot things that you have never noticed.

Waiting lists can be a bit of a lottery, depending on where you live. When I first asked for therapy on the NHS, I was told the waiting list was two months. (Not ideal for someone who'd just had a nervous breakdown.) However, I know friends who received an appointment within three weeks, which is more acceptable. To get an appointment you need to speak to your doctor and request to see an NHS therapist. If you haven't heard anything after two weeks, be sure to chase this up with the surgery.

I gained access to therapy when I became a member of the charity Anxiety UK. At the time of writing a yearly membership costs £30.00. Along with other benefits, members receive access to reduced-cost therapy from approved therapists. The process is simple: a member is required to complete a form, briefly outlining their condition, location and therapy preference. Your doctor's info is also requested, but this is just in case of an emergency. After the form is returned, the member is referred to a suitable therapist, who will be in touch to arrange the initial appointment. This normally takes two weeks. There are different types of therapeutic approach, but the main ones recommended for social anxiety are cognitive behavioural therapy (CBT) and exposure therapy (see pages 63-75). For guidance on choosing a therapist, see the box below.

Choosing the right therapist

Before Anxiety UK 'hooked me up', I decided to pay for therapy myself. I had a savings account and in my desperate state I was willing to pay any amount for help. So I went to see someone on Harley Street, my reason being 'well surely they're the best if their office is on Harley Street'. It was £120 for a 50-minute session. (When did that start happening BTW? Sessions used to be an hour, SO where has the 50-minute thing come from?) Anyway, I was very disappointed with the woman I saw. She seemed distracted and spent more time talking about the services she offered rather than asking about me. On our third session she forgot my name – she called me Catherine (twice) and that was the end of our working relationship!

One of my friends had a similar experience. She had to explain to her therapist the definition of 'introvert' because he'd never heard it before! Not encouraging.

It's important to find a therapist who is right for you. You can start your search with Google, but I would recommend getting a referral via a mental health charity. Once you have a name, research them. Find out their background and experience and if you're not happy, ask for somebody else. The only exception to this is NHS therapy as it works on availability. If you decline one person, it might be weeks until another one is available.

Mental health ambassador Dr Pooky Knightsmith[1] (seriously how cool is that name) recommends that you ask yourself the following: What are your aims and objectives? What is it likely to cost in terms of money and time? Both solid questions. Before investing in a course

---

1   www.inourhands.com/contact

of therapy it's important to assess how much money you can afford and how much time you can realistically devote each week.

During a typical first session you can expect the therapist, counsellor, shrink (whatever you want to call them) to be polite but emotionally docile. They are not there to agree and empathise with you; it's their job to evaluate. For the first ten minutes they should talk about their experience and how they can help. You will then be expected to talk about why you're there. Don't be surprised if this is an emotional experience, so bring tissues! Giving voice to your problems officially makes them real and this can be upsetting, particularly if you've been holding onto them for a while. Just remember, you have every right to be heard.

Consider the following:

✖ Do I feel comfortable with this person?

✖ Do I feel like I can trust them?

✖ Will I be comfortable opening up about my experiences?

✖ At the end of the first session the therapist is likely to ask, 'Would you like to continue working with me?' At this stage you're well within your rights to say, 'I think so, but I would like to take a day to think about it and be sure.' There is no pressure to instantly commit.

✖ You can also ask if your therapist can offer Skype sessions – lots of them do these days, which is great. (Sometimes I really struggled to physically get to sessions because the idea of being in public made my anxiety even worse.)

COGNITIVE BEHAVIOURAL THERAPY

CBT is based on the idea that the way we think about situations can have a direct impact on the way we feel and behave. For example, if you convince yourself that a party is going to be awful, then it will affect the way you behave, such as avoiding people, having bad posture and appearing moody (and who wants to talk to the moody cow hiding in the kitchen!). It's a talking treatment that's specifically designed to help you change the way you think via a series of exercises. In particular, it aims to combat negative and irrational thoughts such as 'Nobody likes you,' 'You're going to make a fool of yourself in front of everyone' and 'You can't cope with anything'.

CBT aims to categorise each negative thought. Here's a key:

✖ *All-or-nothing/black-and-white thinking:* Something is either 100% perfect or it's SHIT. For example, 'That conversation didn't go exactly the way I wanted it to, so it was a failure.' *Really? But so much of it was great – you even made him laugh.* 'NO, it was shit. I've failed.'

✖ *Fortune-telling:* 'The party is going to be awful. Nobody will want to talk to me and I'll have a miserable time.'

✖ *Catastrophising:* (This is my personal favourite.) You think about the worst possible outcome. For example, 'I'm going to stammer in this meeting and I'll humiliate myself. Everybody will think I'm an idiot and I'll never be promoted. I will be miserable forever.' Seriously, sometimes I've actually come up with a contingency plan of how I'm going to behave when it all goes wrong: 'OK, I'll email my boss and the team and say that I wasn't feeling well. Then I'll take some time off to make it seem legit and then I'll leave the country!'

✖ *Mind-reading:* Presuming that you can tell exactly what another person is thinking – and surprise, surprise, it's rarely good. For example, 'Emma looked really bored during our conversation.

She was only talking to me out of pity. She must think I'm the biggest loser in the world.' *Maybe she was tired or thinking about something in her personal life?* 'NO, it was definitely me.'

✖ *Personalising:* Believing that all bad things are directly related to you. For example, 'Sam seemed really moody this morning. I must have done something to annoy him. Maybe I should say something?' *He did mention yesterday that he had a cold – maybe it was that?* 'NO, it's something I've done.'

✖ *Dismissing the positive:* Overlooking any successes in favour of the negatives. For example, 'The food was nice, but I chose the wrong wine and it ruined everything. The whole thing was a failure.' *But you cooked a delicious meal and everybody complimented you on it. It wasn't the wine you originally wanted, but it was still good.* 'NO, it ruined everything.'

There are many more categories that I could mention, but these are the basics. Understanding them will help you to spot them during various exercises.

> **TIP:** Understanding your triggers will allow you to pre-empt your anxiety and tackle it in advance. When I have a presentation coming up at work I prepare both professionally and mentally. When you identify a trigger, jot down the symptoms you experience – both the physical and mental ones. What thoughts pop into your head and how do you feel? This will come in handy for future CBT exercises.

CBT is something that you can do yourself at home, but I would recommend at least three sessions with a therapist as they'll be able to get you on the right track. Also, it's very liberating to vent about what's bothering you to an impartial stranger. They will see things that you don't and offer useful advice. They're being paid to listen to you so there's no element of guilt!

In CBT there are a variety of exercises used to tackle irrational thinking, but my personal favourite is a 'thought chart'. I use it when my mind is flooded with negative thoughts. It's a great way to organise these thoughts and challenge them. There are lots of templates on the internet, but here is my basic method (just write the headings down on a piece of paper or in the notes section of your phone):

Thought chart exercise

Negative thoughts

Write them down clearly:

'Jane thought I was an idiot in that meeting.'

'I'm definitely going to make a fool of myself at the party tonight.'

Emotions

Write down what you feel. (Some templates ask you to 'rate the intensity of the feeling from 1-10, but I've never found that useful. Feel free to add this though.) For example:

Dread, fear, anxiety, stress...

Identify the thinking errors

Have a good look through the negative thoughts list above and see which category they fall into.

'Jane thought I was an idiot in that meeting.' (This is *mind-reading* and *black-and-white thinking*.)

'I'm going to make a fool of myself at the party tonight.' (This is *fortune-telling* and *catastrophising*.)

Is there any evidence to prove that this is true?

To be clear, I mean something concrete. A handy tip to use when challenging a thought is to consider whether it would stand up as evidence in court. For example:

Judge: And how are you certain that your new colleague hates you?

Me: Well, she didn't laugh at my joke and she gave me a funny look yesterday.

Judge: Are you taking the piss?

New thought

Now you have identified the thinking errors and reviewed the evidence, re-write the thoughts with a new rational commentary:

'Jane thought I was an idiot in that meeting.'

Sadly none of us can read minds. If we could, we'd all be superheroes! You have no idea what she was thinking and the chance that she thinks you're an idiot because of one thing you said is highly unlikely. She might not even have been listening. Think about it: how often do you drift off during a meeting?

'I'm going to make a fool of myself at the party tonight.'

This is a very bold claim! Again, nobody can predict the future. You're being tricked by your emotions into believing something that hasn't even happened yet. Sure, OK, you might not be a social butterfly tonight and that's fine. However, unless you plan on streaking around the room with a plant on your head, I doubt you'll make a fool of yourself.

TIP: One of the main drawbacks of CBT is that it's time-consuming. It can take a while to master all of the 'thinking error' categories. One solution is to write them out in your own words so they are more specific to you and therefore more memorable.

EXPOSURE THERAPY

Exposure therapy has been incredibly useful for me. It's a more aggressive form of treatment as it involves deliberately triggering an anxious episode, but in my experience the results are long lasting. However, I wouldn't recommend this approach until you have started to deal with your inner demons and feel more stable.

The basic principle is very simple. You expose yourself to situations that make you feel uncomfortable, experience anxiety and work through it until you become desensitised to the situation. Now, this doesn't mean if you're afraid of heights then jump out of a plane! Or if public speaking makes you feel sick then arrange to lead a conference! If anything, this is the fastest way to traumatise yourself! The key is *small doses*: do things a little at a time and build up slowly.

This will secure a more solid foundation that your brain will accept and remember.

The basics

Exposure therapy involves triggering an anxious episode or panic attack, so that you can learn how to deal with your anxiety in a more positive way. Basically, it's practising, so when the real thing comes along you'll be better prepared.

In order to progress you need to accept/embrace how anxiety or panic makes you feel, rather than trying to fight it. It's not an easy thing to do (complete understatement), but it is doable. Don't be disappointed if your first few attempts go tits up. On my first attempt (in a restaurant), I literally stood and said 'nope', then left the building!

Panic and anxiety are not pleasant sensations, so it's natural to want to avoid them. However, by leaving the situation, in essence you're confirming to the brain (the amygdala) that it was right to trigger an attack, because you were in a dangerous situation. The amygdala learns by association, so it will automatically trigger an attack in future. I wasn't in any danger in the restaurant, but by legging it out the door I convinced my brain that I was.

So – as bloody awful as it may seem – accepting the attack and all the nasty feelings that come with it is the better way to deal with it. The amygdala can only learn when you're in a state of fear (typical, huh), so staying put and facing the situation will give it the chance to understand that you're NOT in danger and therefore an attack will not be triggered to the same extent next time.

Now the big question is...how do I accept an attack? When I first asked this question I compared it to accepting being punched in the stomach. How is it possible?!

David Carbonell (AKA 'My God') came up with a strategy. The website[2] might seem basic design-wise, but his content is pure gold! I have adapted his process, AWARE, for two reasons: 1) I hate acronyms; 2) I really don't think the 'E' is needed, but you'll have to check out his website and form your own opinions. So, here is my version:

Greet the attack

Acknowledge in this moment that the panic/anxiety is starting to build and it's making you feel afraid. Don't try to fight it or force it to go away (that will only make it worse). Instead, say to yourself, 'OK, here we go, it's starting. Panic cannot hurt me or make me go insane – that's impossible. It can only make me feel distressed and uncomfortable for a while.' Let it wash over you like a wave or an unfair lecture for something that wasn't your fault. Stop resisting physically and mentally – just let it come. Sometimes I say to myself, 'Oh, hi Panic, I was waiting for you.' Welcome it.

---

2   www.anxietycoach.com/overcoming-panic-attacks.html

This will initially feel worse and probably more emotional, as your brain thinks you're ignoring the danger signs. So when it does, don't freak out. It's a good thing, it means it's working!

Wait

If you're anything like me, panic temporarily robs you of your ability to think straight. That's why we do stupid things like run away or hide in toilets! So when I say 'Wait', I mean 'Stay where you are' (count to ten if it helps). Remaining where you are will give your rational side time to kick in and access the situation before you do anything.

You will most definitely have an overwhelming urge to flee the situation, because, again, the amygdala thinks you're in danger. 'What the f**k are you doing? We're going to die. You need to get out NOW!' This is how mine speaks to me. However, staying put will help to further educate it.

Comfort

Now we need to help the body to feel more comfortable because it's probably in agony! Start by clenching your muscles really tight for five seconds and then releasing. This exercise is a classic, so apologies if you've heard it before...but it's a very effective way to increase oxygen levels and help reduce palpitations and shortness of breath.

Belly breathing is much easier to explain by physically demonstrating it, but I'll give it a go here anyway!

1. Exhale – do a big sigh like you're really fed up. This will relax the muscles. You only need to do this once before taking the first breath.

2. Slowly breathe in through your nose, but as you do so, push your stomach out as far as you can. If it helps, place one hand on your stomach to make sure that you're doing it correctly.

3. Hold for a few seconds.

4. As you breathe out, slowly suck your stomach back in.

5. Repeat this three times, or more if needed.

Get back in the moment

If you're in a meeting, listen intently to what is being said, or ask a question. If you're on public transport, smile at another passenger, or ask the time.

Be prepared for a re-run

If the panic starts building again, no worries – this is completely normal. Just repeat the process again.

✖   ✖   ✖

Now we've covered the prep work, we can begin the next stage. Think of the main area that provokes an anxious reaction. It could be parties, work, driving or even a specific person. It really doesn't matter.

Write a list of ten steps, starting with the easiest one first and the hardest last. This will be your 'exposure challenges list'. Tailor it to suit your exact situation. You can have more than one situation if you struggle in multiple areas.

I used to (and sometimes still do) have anxiety or panic attacks before meetings at work. By way of example, here is my list for dealing with that:

1. Sit in my living room, close my eyes and imagine being in a meeting. Imagine everything from the room to the people in it.

2. Sit at my desk at work and imagine being in a meeting.

3. Go and sit in a meeting room on my own for five minutes. Leave the door open.

4. Go and sit in a meeting room on my own for five minutes. Close the door.

5. Go and sit in a meeting room on my own, close the door and imagine speaking. Say a sentence out loud and imagine others looking at you.

6. Sit in a meeting room with a friend and chat casually about anything.

7. Sit in a meeting room with a friend and discuss something work-related.

8. At home, sit around a table with a family member or partner and pretend to be in an actual meeting. (Warn them in advance that it's an exercise and give them topics to discuss.) Sit there for ten minutes.

9. Attend a real meeting, but inform your boss beforehand that you'll be a casual observer.

10. Attend a real meeting and contribute once.

This example is very specific to a problem that I had and I appreciate that it might seem boring or even ridiculous. But it's really important to build things up slowly.

OTHER AVENUES OF THERAPY AND EXERCISES

Mindfulness meditation

This has recently become a hot topic, with Headspace being the leading app supplier. Headspace provides a free step-by-step programme of ten-minute sessions. Each session includes basic breathing techniques and guidance on how to focus the mind's attention on the body. Some people rave about it, whereas others aren't keen. The basic idea of mindfulness is to allow the brain to be present in the moment rather than thinking about the past or future, and to become more aware of the body and how it's feeling. I pretty much spend my life in the past and future, I'm either thinking about what I need to do later or reliving a previous event. So I was very interested in this concept.

In all honesty, I've had mixed results. The exercises require the user to focus on their breathing (which can make me hyperventilate!). Also, the idea of 'being present' was completely foreign to my brain, so it didn't accept this easily. I often found myself 'wandering off' and thinking about other things by accident! However, as the app explains, this is all perfectly normal. After using Headspace for seven days I did start to notice a difference. I now use it three days a week in the mornings, to set me up for the day. I must admit it's nice to spend ten minutes completely with myself without feeling guilty. The basic package is free, but in order to unlock the rest of the exercises you have to subscribe and pay a monthly fee.

Although Headspace is the most publicised tool on the market, there are also a variety of books and online resources[3] that teach mindfulness.

> **TIP:** It tends to work better if you have a general f**k-it attitude, rather than expecting too much. So try and think, 'If it works, great; if not, then no worries.' Give it a try for ten days before making any decisions.

---

3   For more information visit the 'BeMindful' website at http://bemindful.co.uk

Distraction

Sometimes in life we all need a nice distraction to shift the brain away from negative thoughts. Distraction techniques are incredibly useful and can be as simple or as complicated as you like. Here are some ideas:

✖ Think of as many girls' names, boys' names, bands, countries, animals or swear words (whatever you like) as you can that begin with the letter 'A'.

✖ Try to remember all of the characters in *Game of Thrones*. First name and last.

✖ Mentally walk from your house to the centre of town. Visualise each street and all the moments/ shops on the way. I use this one if I'm having trouble sleeping. It's like an adventure from the safety of your bed!

✖ App games are great and often free to download.

✖ Audio books are also good.

Positive refocus exercise

The brain rarely focuses on the present (unless you're being mugged) - it's usually somewhere in the past or future. The amygdala is very theatrical. Mine likes to create a teen drama worthy of its own TV series, complete with all the scenarios that could go wrong. Every episode ends the same way: I make a fool of myself.

While they're easy to indulge in, these 'false premonitions' of how an event will go are very damaging. Thoughts trigger emotional responses, so not only will you feel nervous but also like you've already had a terrible time, which is mental as it hasn't even happened yet!

The way to combat this is to take control of your imagination and re-write the script. Take a moment and imagine the event going really well. Imagine people smiling and some of the things you will say. This will flood your body with positive emotions and give you an extra boost of confidence.

Crafty business

Being creative is an excellent way to distract the brain in a positive and productive way. Having a project to focus on will keep your hands busy and your mind from wandering. Writing, knitting, cooking, gardening, creating a collage... There are so many options to choose from. (They are great fun too!)

Anxiety first-aid kit

I'm a fan of a personalised first-aid kit. Basically, fill
it with treats and activities that are relevant to you.
The only rule is that you can only delve into it when
you need a boost. It's a reward for getting through
the day or a difficult situation. Mine includes: a nice
bottle of wine (obviously), endless bags of Maltesers,
posh bubble bath, Top Trumps, a puzzle book, at least
three novels, a historical documentary box set (don't
judge, I'm a huge history geek) and nail varnish. Stock
up on goodies. Your kit doesn't need to be expensive,
but it has to include things that will make you smile.

Animal loving

In my opinion there is no love more pure than that of
an animal. I got my dog Rigby nine months into my
recovery and she's been a key player in keeping my
mental health steady ever since. (Despite the initial 'Oh

my God how am I supposed to take
care of her – I can't even take care
of myself!') When you're having a
terrible day and your anxiety feels
all-consuming, having a snuggle
with your pet can really help
to calm everything down. This
calming effect isn't limited to
dogs. Cats can also be soothing
companions and they're much
less demanding, both physically

and financially, than dogs. Purring is one of the most relaxing sounds ever (in my opinion)! However, cats do tend to bring home the odd dead bird as a present... so not the right pet if you're squeamish.

You don't have to explain anything to a pet. You don't have to apologise for burdening them with your troubles or feel stupid in their presence. You can be whatever and they'll love you all the same. It's also nice to have company when you can't sleep.

However, taking on an animal can be expensive. Do not bring one into your home unless you can take care of it properly. This means food, healthcare, grooming, toys, poop management and arranging care for during the day (dogs should not be alone for more than three hours). You can see these considerations are close to my heart! If you have a full-time job then, on average, you should expect to pay £5000 a year to keep a dog (pedigree or mongrel), the majority of which goes on day care. If you work from home or part time the cost is reduced to just over £1000. Dog-walking is a bloody lucrative industry! Cats are much cheaper because day care is not required – £1000 a year is the general estimate. If you can do all these things, an animal can inject some real positivity and comfort into your life.[4]

---

4   If you can't afford to keep a dog, then websites such as www.borrowmydoggy.com are great. You pay a small yearly fee to become a member and then you can interact with local dog owners who are looking for sitters. You get cuddles without any of the financial responsibility! Again, there are strict rules and the care of any dog should be taken seriously.

Chapter 3

SCHOOL AND UNIVERSITY LIFE

SCHOOL DAYS

They say that your school years are the best of your life. Well far be it from me to call anyone a liar, but they must've been f**king joking! I still have nightmares about that time.

Think about it from a literary perspective: David Copperfield was beaten, Jane Eyre was made to stand on a chair for hours, and Harry Potter...well, he was attacked practically every other day by one thing or another. There is no need to despair though. It might be a challenging time, but it doesn't last forever and these days you don't have to suffer in silence. Many schools are more clued up on mental health and the pressures placed on young people. For example, a friend of mine is a teacher and one of her students wrote on a mock exam paper: 'I can't handle the test environment. How am I going to cope in the actual exam?' She took this very seriously and had a chat with the student after class. Together they worked out a plan whereby he could practise being in an exam setting. This mini form of exposure therapy helped to prepare him for the real thing. Charities such as Student Minds are also on hand to offer help and advice. As mental health campaigner Natasha Devon (2015) pointed out, 'You cannot apply an adult amount of pressure to a child's brain and expect them to cope.' The education system is starting to take this seriously.

Regrettably, mental health and emotional wellbeing were not considered during my years in the education system. I found secondary school in particular very difficult and I can't really sugar coat it. For the first time in my life I was forced to behave in a way that was deemed 'desirable' rather than what felt natural to me.

Constant group work, speaking out in class and reading aloud were all activities that 'normal' and happy children do. In contrast, I preferred working on my own and presenting ideas to smaller groups rather than to a class of 30 hungry and cruel teenagers. It also didn't help that I froze whenever a teacher spoke to me. Seriously I'd be lucky if I could remember my own name!

It wasn't an environment that got the best out of me, and sadly many of my teachers were clueless about my discomfort.

Here's an example from my school report in geography:

> Claire is a shy and deeply reserved girl. She doesn't answer questions without being directly prompted and she doesn't enjoy sharing her work with the class. She also seems to spend lots of time daydreaming, which is a concern. She needs to make a special effort to come out of her shell if she wants to do well.

Notice that the report makes no reference to the actual quality of the work I produced (I was mostly an A/B grade student). It only mentions my personality, which seems bizarre.

Teachers generally assumed that because I daydreamed and was quiet in class, there was something wrong with me. I remember a maths teacher once referred to me as being 'a bit thick' in a fit of temper. Classmates delighted in these labels and used them to berate me constantly.

Despite the fact that I now have a Bachelor's degree, a Master's degree and a good job, in my darker moments I still see myself as being 'thick'. That's the thing about labels – they're bloody sticky! Although the harsh words from classmates stopped years ago, the damage has been done.

Secondary school was also the time in my life where my confidence in both my appearance and personality was severely attacked. Fellow students were more than happy to inform me that I was ugly and weird. In particular, I was criticised for being skinny, pale and flat-chested. As an adult, I would've told them all to f**k off, but as a young and impressionable teenage girl I accepted every word they said as gospel and spent years investing in fake tan and padded bras! I also tried to dye my hair on numerous occasions. I thought that if I could just be blonde, tanned and have bigger boobs then everything would be OK. I grew up in the footballers' wives era – looking like a WAG* was the ultimate goal. All photographs from this period have subsequently been destroyed!

So yes, in a nutshell it was quite a horrible time and by the age of 15 I'd developed some very physical symptoms of anxiety, as I described in the Introduction. In class I would blush deeply every time I was spoken to directly, and the more I became stressed about people noticing it, the more I blushed. I also had quite bad tremors and hated raising my hand in case this was spotted. I didn't realise it at the time, but it was the beginning of a lengthy battle with anxiety. Like most people would have done, I tried to ignore it and hoped that I would get better as I grew up. I didn't understand what was happening to me.

It was at university that I finally realised I wasn't weird or different – I was actually just an introvert!

---

* wives or girlfriends of famous footballers.

Introvert

The following is a mini profile of your typical introvert:

✖ They prefer to listen, rather than dominate conversations. (This doesn't make them shy.)

✖ They prefer smaller groups and intimate conversations to huge group activities.

✖ They require 'down time/quiet time'. Their brains can become overstimulated and need time to recharge. Personally, I only have a limited amount of energy that I can 'give' to people each day, and once that's maxed out, I'm done. If I can't recharge, I become grumpy and emotional. In contrast, extroverts need to be around others to recharge.

I read Susan Cain's book *Quiet: The Power of Introverts in a World That Can't Stop Talking* and the penny finally dropped. It was OK to be an introvert! It doesn't make you a pushover or weak. In fact, some of the world's most powerful people are/were self-confessed introverts:

✖ Barack Obama

✖ Abraham Lincoln

✖ Charles Dickens

✖ Nelson Mandela.

If only I had bloody realised this when I was at school! It was perfectly OK to be an introvert and in many ways it's a great thing. Difference doesn't equal strange, and I learned that as I got older.

THE UNIVERSITY YEARS

University was one of the biggest culture shocks I've ever experienced. I went from being overly controlled and regimented at school to suddenly being handed the reins of power. Living away from home, being expected to organise my own timetable, no formal introductions to classmates... From all rules to no rules – talk about whiplash! All of my closest friends from home were now scattered across the country. I had to start from scratch.

Once again, I was told by my careers advisor, 'University will be your finest years. You'll make friends for life and develop into a well-rounded adult.' What she failed to tell me was that I'd be really poor and was expected to live in squalor and be constantly full of energy and 'ultra-fun' in order to fit in. Now to be clear, I love a good night out. Drinking

cocktails, chatting with friends and, more importantly, dancing! (Seriously, I'll tear up any dance floor.) But even at the age of 18 I couldn't do this every night – I was knackered! I found the university social scene to be really challenging. There was so much pressure to be relevant and interesting. Having one-night stands, staying up for two days straight and taking cocaine were the norm. I did none of these things, so I was very much out of my depth.

Alcohol and caffeine

One evening I found this magical substance that suppressed all of my anxiety and made me feel super-confident. Naturally, I'm talking about alcohol. It was a miracle. Finally I had found my cure! After a few drinks of liquid courage I was a different person. I could talk to strangers, relax and be 'normal' for a few hours. If only that was the end of the story, huh? Me and my bottle of wine rode off into the sunset together. Alas, while alcohol provides short-term relief

from anxiety, it is not a long-term solution because...well, there's a catch, right? That's life!

I became reliant on it to help me get through social events and even started having a drink before I went out. (Don't worry, this isn't the part where I tell you that I became an alcoholic, and spent three years clutching a bottle of vodka in the gutter.)

I really wanted to believe that alcohol was the answer to all my anxiety problems because it had such an immediate positive effect. Whenever I read an article suggesting that alcohol made things worse, I didn't believe it. Surely it was just the government's way to stop students from binge drinking?

However, by the time I reached 23, I couldn't ignore the signs any more. Too much booze DOES in fact increase anxiety symptoms. First of all, it makes your brain lazy and reduces its ability to cope with stress. I mean, if you have a miracle cure, why not use it for everything? Your brain never has to face fear alone again. This is certainly not a good habit to get into. Your brain is your most valued tool and should be kept strong.

Hangovers are the main area of destruction. Many young adults (including me back then) don't realise that hangovers not only affect you physically (being sick, headaches and generally wishing you were dead);

they also have a massive impact on your emotions and mental health. Everybody gets that feeling of self-loathing the day after a heavy drinking session, but if you suffer from anxiety then it's likely to be much worse. Alcohol messes with the serotonin levels and other hormones in the brain. Remember how important serotonin is from Chapters 1 and 2? Well drinking essentially f**ks it up, particularly as the alcohol starts to wear off. I found that I was staying in bed all day with hangovers and I felt miserable. Alcohol also heightened my sense of paranoia – and believe me that's something that didn't need a boost! I would obsess about the previous night's events. Had I made a fool of myself? Why wasn't my friend texting me back? I began checking social media sites, furiously scanning for any embarrassing photos.

Alcohol also makes you crave foods that are really bad for you. Sugar, salt and saturated fats are among the biggest culprits. We know they're bad for the body, but large amounts of such foods are bad for the brain, too. An excess of sugar can cause an adrenalin spike.

Hangovers make you feel tired, which leads me nicely on to the next substance I discovered: caffeine. Again, what a miracle bitter dark liquid! If wine chilled me out, then coffee hyped me up. I could go to lectures wide awake after four hours' rest and

write essays when I should've been sleeping. I took Pro Plus and drank Red Bull too when I really needed a boost. Looking back now, I cringe – what a stupid cow I was! I'm sure that this is fairly obvious, but just to clarify: **RED FLAG ONE:** caffeine is a stimulant that affects the central nervous system. **RED FLAG TWO:** caffeine increases the amount of adrenalin in the body. It's essentially like pouring fuel onto a fire. One cup is OK, five is not! Twenty minutes later, when you find yourself shaking with a pounding heart, trust me it's the caffeine.

> **TIP:** Alcohol and caffeine are fine. I'd be a hypocrite if I said that I didn't indulge. The key word to remember is 'MODERATION'. It's true that alcohol can take the edge of nerves. But too much will only deplete your serotonin levels and increase your anxiety symptoms the following day.

EXAMS

In 2015, ChildLine received 34,000 calls from teenagers struggling to cope with exam-related stress (Adams 2015). I can relate to this, and if I'd have known that you could ring someone, then I might've given it a go!

When I was applying for university, it was sold as being the most important thing in the world. So, for an impressionable and sensitive person like me, this triggered a volume of negative overthinking. I needed to get into university, excel in every class and then get my degree. If I slipped up even once, I wouldn't get my degree, I wouldn't be able to get a job and would end up begging on the street. My parents would be devastated (they never ever mentioned this – I just assumed it) and I would be a shame on the family. That's a lot of pressure to put on oneself!

On top of this, I felt pressure from my school to excel. In assembly the headteacher addressed the final-year students and spoke about the all-important 'league table'. Our school regularly secured a place in the top five positions and he reminded us of our duty to 'do well and not let the school down'. I was very aware that I was expected to achieve my predicted grades and I didn't want to disappoint. After all, schools are a business to a certain extent – the terminology is just different. Sales people have targets to hit and so do teachers. Sales want to attract customers and schools want to attract better students. But where do we draw the line?

At university, learning was a different battleground to anything I'd ever experienced. Revision was hard enough at school, but at least I could ask the teacher for guidance, whereas now I was expected to study completely solo and any direction should come from a library book. Picture this scene:

Lecturer:	During this semester we have studied eight topics and the final exam will consist of questions with regard to two of those topics. I would suggest that you revise all eight thoroughly.
Me:	Have you seen the paper?
Lecturer:	Yes, of course.
Me:	Couldn't you narrow it down to maybe four topics? I'm not asking for the questions, of course, but it seems pointless to revise all eight when only two will be in the exam.
Lecturer:	I'm surprised you would ask. Any academic would be happy to revise all eight.

Oops, clearly I don't think like an academic! Seriously though, is it me or does that just seem ridiculous?

On top of revision- and essay-related stress I was also afraid to speak up in tutorials, through a fear of looking like an idiot. It's true, I didn't use traditional academic language and I probably asked stupid questions. So I never said a word and spent most of the time worrying about whether the tutor would ask me a question. In reality, I should've thought, 'F**k it, I'm paying a small fortune for this, so I'm going to do and say as I please!' But, as always, the pressure to fit in and look normal got the better of me. Social anxiety thrives in environments where difference is not encouraged.

Getting a good mark in every exam became imperative to me – it was my whole life. I had to prove that I wasn't an idiot, even if it meant memorising books by heart! My legs were physically shaking as I climbed the stairs to the results boards at the end of the first term. (That was a nice touch BTW: let's advertise everyone's results on a board for the whole world to see. Who needs privacy?) I always did well, but the fear and adrenalin wouldn't dissipate for days afterwards. This wasn't a new phenomenon by any means – it happened after my GCSEs and A-levels, too.

If I could go back my younger self, I'd give her some advice on what qualifications actually count for in the wider scheme of things, to help reduce the exam anxiety within! Apologies...these are all geared towards the UK, but I hope if you're not based here you can work out your country's equivalent:

- ✖ *GCSEs:* Don't worry too much as they don't count for anything in the adult world. Just aim for Cs – this will get you into college.

- ✖ *A-levels:* These will get you into university. THAT'S IT. So again, just aim for what you need. If you don't get straight As, it really isn't a big deal in the long run.

- ✖ *Bachelor's degree:* This is when it gets more serious – you're actually paying for your own education now, so don't f**k about. First year you can afford to just pass, but second and third year are important.

✗ *Master's degree:* Seriously, don't f**k about - this is well expensive!

Try your best, but don't drive yourself into the ground. Perspective is an important thing. Sure, it might be embarrassing for a day or two that you didn't get straight As, but in a week it won't matter any more. Value your wellbeing over pride.

Disclaimer: I am not encouraging students to be lazy and reject their educational responsibilities. Education is very important as it's something that we should value. But we should also value our health. It all comes down to finding the right balance.

TIP: Tell someone!

✗ If you're really struggling and there's a teacher or professor that you trust, then arrange a meeting to discuss your issues. Maybe you can't bear the idea of giving a presentation in class? Perhaps alternative arrangements can be made. Or perhaps you just need to tell someone how you're feeling.

✗ Many universities have designated support groups for students with mental health issues. Peer-to-peer mentoring is on the rise in education, so do some research.

FACEBOOK AND ME

At around the age of 18, I finally embraced Facebook (I was a bit of a technophobe). It was one the best and worst things I've ever done. I have a love/hate relationship with social media. It's at the same time wonderful and monstrous, informative and crushing, liberating and oppressive. I can still remember my first Facebook profile...filled with information that didn't reflect my personality at all. I cringe thinking about how many drafts I wrote for the 'about me' section. At that age I had no bloody clue who I was! But according to my profile I was essentially a character from a TV series. She didn't exist. The problem with creating a fictional character is that you can't control reality or censor other people's interaction, and this could jeopardise all of your hard work. I became obsessed with controlling my 'online image'. Photo tagging was my worst nightmare. I was very insecure about my looks, and photos used to be a major cause of distress. I couldn't control how I looked and would therefore be held hostage to somebody else's camera. When the notification 'somebody tagged in you six photos' appeared, my heart would sink. I desperately clicked to review the damage and de-tag any monstrosities. It all stems back to my obsession with being 'perfect', and this naturally applied to my appearance. I wanted to look like Keira Knightley, Kate Moss or Zooey Deschanel... not myself! Although in fairness, these women don't actually exist either. It's all a photoshopped illusion of perfection (but I'll save that rant for another time).

Social media

These days, if you don't have a social media account, you don't technically exist. Facebook, Twitter, Instagram, Snapchat, Pinterest – there are a whole variety to choose from, depending on your needs/snooping requirements. Think about it: how often have you looked up a potential new boss on LinkedIn? (I was devastated when I realised that this function wasn't anonymous!) Facebook stalking your latest crush is practically common practice. Or how many followers does your new friend have on Twitter?

However, as with many things in life, there is a dark side to such access. Do you really want to know that your ex isn't in fact dead (as you'd originally hoped) but is dating a supermodel? Or that some colleagues went to the local pub without you? The problem with this is a lack of context, and without admitting that you stalked someone, you will not receive this precious context. So it's natural to presume that your ex has the perfect life and your colleagues hate you. Talk about anxiety-provoking! I once spent an evening trying to work out why an old colleague was in the pub with our manager when I hadn't been invited. It turns out that they were both in the same place by chance and my colleague had conveniently updated her status to be misleading. Still, I foolishly spent hours worrying. Did my manager not like me? Was I boring? Would I get fired for being boring?!! Sometimes ignorance really is bliss.

Oh, and don't even get me started on the popularity contest that social media encourages. Twitter in particular is brutal. How many followers do you have? I thought I'd be happy when I hit 1000 – but I just wanted even more. Also, I'd be lying if I said that I don't feel the pain of rejection whenever I lose someone. How could they 'unfollow' me? What did I do wrong? I thought I was freaking hilarious!

Instagram is the worst for making a person feel ugly or that their life is inadequate. As much as I like beauty bloggers, I don't constantly need to see the mountains of free stuff that they get sent, beautifully displayed on an oak wooden floor with scattered flowers and a vintage filter!

Also, when did we stop smiling in photos? Seriously, when did that happen? Sometimes I catch myself 'posing' and I'm like 'WTF, this isn't a red carpet, I'm having a good time with my friends!'

Here are my general social media guidelines:

✖ Don't check Facebook on a Friday or Saturday night if you're at home alone and feeling rubbish. Why do it to yourself? I often leave my phone in another room.

✖ When you lose a Twitter follower, I'm afraid it's because they 'just weren't that into you' – so move on.

✖ Make sure that your Facebook is set to 'private' (no brainer). We wouldn't want your new employer to see that photo from the pole-dancing evening.

✖ **DON'T CLICK ON YOUR EX'S PROFILE**, especially when drunk or alone. Watch a Disney film instead! (We both know that you will anyway.) Just be prepared for the worst and try to remember the phrase 'lack of context'. That bitch he's got his arm round could just be a family member... Unlikely, but it could be!

✖ Don't ever take naked photos of yourself... PERIOD. They'll end up online. They just will.

DEALING WITH EMOTIONAL SCARS

There's nothing I can do about the past, so I try not to spend time thinking about those years. I do sometimes wonder if educators realise how much of an impact they can have on a child's life. Not all children are the same, and surely differences should be celebrated (unless they're taking drugs in class) rather than challenged and criticised? However, research suggests that schools are starting to take the mental wellbeing of children more seriously. I can definitely sympathise with teachers, too...an endless workload, the pressure of school inspections, parents' evenings, and now they have to find time for mental health. It's not an easy job and they can only work with the resources that a school provides. Perhaps I was an oversensitive girl? I'm sure that many adults had a hellish time at school and still managed to brush it off and forget. But unfortunately not everybody is born with the innate ability to do this with ease. Secondary school was my trigger and any environment that reminds me of school immediately sets off my anxiety.

TIPS

✖ If you have scars from the past, then bare them. We spend so much time trying to ignore pain, when sometimes the best way to heal is to release it.

✖ You can do this privately or with a friend/family member. Just get the experiences out of your memory bank and into the cold light of day.

Thoughts automatically trigger emotional responses. For example, when I think about my school maths class I feel embarrassed and sad. I was a 'loser and weird'. Or at least, that's how my brain has chosen to remember it. That's the problem with memories – they can become skewed. So I desperately try to think about something else, which helps in the short term but doesn't deal with the root of the memory.

Embrace and let go exercise

One day I wrote down my thoughts and included everything from a scene at school: what was said, how it made me feel and the reactions of others. I adapted the CBT thought chart technique that I mentioned in Chapter 2. (This exercise is rather lengthy so try to stay with me!)

Picturing the scene

It's a mid-morning maths class and I'm staring out the window, daydreaming. Suddenly I hear my name shouted.

Mrs Smith: Claire!

Me: *Stunned, I turn and look at her*

Mrs Smith: Daydreaming again. Well go on, what's the answer?

Me: *Starts blushing* I'm sorry, Miss. I didn't hear the question.

Mrs Smith: Stand up! *She shouts* Stand up immediately!

Me: *Blushes even more, starts trembling and stands up slowly*

Classmate: Look! She's gone bright red!

Rest of the class: *Start laughing*

Mrs Smith: We're all waiting. Come on, what's the answer?

Me: I'm sorry Miss, I didn't...

Mrs Smith: You didn't hear the question. To be honest, Claire, I sometimes wonder if you daydream so much because you're a bit thick!

Rest of class: *Laugh more*

Mrs Smith: Sit down, you silly girl.

I can feel the tears burning in my eyes, as I stare at my text book. My friend Lisa asks if I'm OK and I just nod. The boy I really fancy is in class too. I'll never be able to talk to him again.

Experiencing the memory

How do I feel about this scene in the present?

- ✖ *Feelings:* 'Humiliated, exposed and pathetic.'

- ✖ *Thoughts:* 'It proves that I was never a normal child and I'm still not today. I was destined to be an outsider without normal social skills. I don't know why I even try to deal with my anxiety because it's clearly ingrained in me. I'm just a freak.'

I think we can agree that it is clearly an emotionally loaded memory – a 60-second interaction from 15 years ago that my brain still clings onto.

When I did this exercise, I gave myself a good two minutes to fully experience the memory and allow the emotions to wash over me. It was unpleasant, but it also felt liberating. Rather than fighting the emotions I was finally embracing them.

Challenging negativity

Next, I identified the thinking errors and challenged the negative thoughts:

✖ 'It proves that I wasn't a normal child and I'm still not a normal person today.' *That's very 'black-and-white thinking'. What is the definition of a 'normal person' anyway? I don't break the law, I have a happy family, a good job and friends. What's not normal about that?!*

✖ 'I don't know why I even try to deal with my anxiety, because it's clearly ingrained in me. I'm just a freak.' *Maybe I'm personalising the memory too much. Yes, it was embarrassing, and yes, Mrs Smith shouldn't have spoken to me that way. But she might've been tired or in a bad mood and accidently took it out on me. It doesn't prove without a shadow of a doubt that I'm a freak. I just got unlucky. I had lots of friends who comforted me after the experience and agreed that I was victimised. It didn't prove anything about me then or now. It was just a shit day.*

As I said, the activity sounds lengthy, but once you get the hang of it, it's simple. I spent nearly two hours writing down all the horrible things that had happened to me at secondary school. I wrote down cruel names I'd been called, times I'd been betrayed by friends, and unfair punishment from teachers. I wrote everything out and I let myself feel that pain because I owed it to that girl, and then I said out loud (privately), 'F**k it. I'm a different person now and I accept who I am.' It's almost a process of exorcism. Feel the pain, embrace it, enjoy it and then let it go.

So why not give this a try when you have time? Really think about those emotionally charged memories and explore them. Remember the five steps:

1. Write out the scene in full.

2. How did it make you feel and what thoughts popped into your head?

3. Feel it for two minutes.

4. Pick out the key thoughts and challenge them via the CBT exercise.

5. Let it go. (Listen to the *Frozen* song if it helps.)

Chapter 4

MY BIG
BREAK(DOWN)

Modern young professionals feel the pressure to achieve a lot at an early age. You only need to look at the current role models: the Kardashians, the stars of reality TV shows such as *Made in Chelsea* or *Jersey Shore,* or even beauty bloggers and fashion bloggers like Zoella and Tavi Gevinson (she broke into fashion age 12...when I was still reading Roald Dahl and seeing how many Maltesers I could fit in my mouth!).

Rather than thinking about what we want and what makes us happy, we spend our time focusing on what we 'should' be doing. I pushed myself to a nervous breakdown by setting endless tasks and deadlines for myself.

I've always had a compulsive fear of mediocracy. I never thought that I was better than anyone else (quite the opposite), but I wanted to 'do things' with my life and I wanted to achieve. Being 'successful' was extremely important to me, although I never once stopped to ask why. I had my head in a book most of the time, so I was bound to be a dreamer. I also got bored easily (still do), so I constantly looked for new ways to stimulate my brain.

As a teenager I realised quickly that according to the standards of contemporary culture, I wasn't beautiful, rich, or musically gifted enough to be on *The X Factor*. So I would need to rely on my brain to get me places. It's not that I didn't love my home town – I still miss it even now – I just knew that I wanted something different.

I would get frustrated with myself. Why couldn't I just be happy with what I had? Why was that never enough? I'll let you know when I figure that one out.

To say that I had an intense plan to achieve is an understatement. I'm a perfectionist and I obsess! Teachers used to call me 'overly conscientious'. They had no f**king idea! It started around the age of 14. I was unhappy with my appearance and I didn't stand out personality-wise. But then we were also fed the idea that if you just work hard enough, you can achieve *anything*. I remember reading a quote by author and motivational speaker Jim Rohn (2014): 'If you really want to do something, you will find a way.' Not sure how I feel about that these days. Does this statement include becoming more famous than Justin Bieber or being the next Emperor of China? But as a teen this idea became my driving force.

I put myself under tremendous pressure to do well at school, college and then university. I had to prove to myself and the world that I wasn't an idiot and that I could be a success. It turns out that impressing oneself is nigh impossible (it's still a work in progress).

GETTING MY MASTER'S DEGREE

Whilst completing my MA in Publishing, I worked full time in a job that I absolutely *hated*. I was a receptionist at a solicitor's in town and the environment was toxic, being shouted at 24/7 by an endless parade of angry people in suits. In many ways it was an extension of school because the abuse was equally as bad. 'Claire, where are my f**king car keys?', one suit screamed at me. I was scrambling around his office like a squirrel stuck in a pedal bin looking for those bloody keys. He casually emerged ten minutes later with them in his hand. He'd left them in the toilets.

But the money was good and I needed it to fund my degree. Also, there was a really fancy coffee machine and sometimes we got free sandwiches! So I kept smiling and turning up each day. They wouldn't break me (I'd do that myself eventually).

I was the only person on the MA course who had a job at the same time as studying. The sheer volume of work meant that after a shift I would write essays in the evenings and then on weekends. Looking back, it was ridiculous - I should've completed the degree part time. But I'm impatient - I tend to want things yesterday, no matter the cost.

I used my annual leave to complete an internship. That's right, no holidays in the sun for me! I don't say this with superiority or pride - looking back, I think I was an idiot! What kind of maniac would put themselves through that amount of strain? And for what?

During this period I also broke up with my boyfriend of four years. My first experience of love. He was in a band and they were totally going to be famous. (Oh dear God, they were shit. But I got to stand backstage at gigs, which made me feel cool...even if it was just the local youth centre!) We broke up because he cheated - TWICE. I probably should've ended it much sooner. Deep down I knew he wasn't good for me, but I just ignored it. See, the mammalian part of the brain tends to be stubborn when it comes to control. I remember the night when we finally broke up. It was 4am and I just nipped downstairs for a glass of water. I checked my phone and found out from Facebook (classy) that he'd done it again. So I booted him out of my life for good. Two weeks later he drunkenly climbed on the roof, carrying what I assume were flowers from our garden, in an attempt to win me back (surprisingly it didn't work).

By the time my dissertation was due, I'd lost a stone in weight and looked terminally ill. The night before it had to be handed in, I staggered into my parents' bedroom and announced, 'If you don't help me, I think I'm going to smash my head through the computer screen.' My dad had to take the following day off work to drive me to university. I hadn't slept in 48 hours and could barely think straight, let alone drive a car!

Afterwards, I caught a terrible cold and was in bed for a week. Most people go out celebrating after handing in their dissertation. I remember crawling into bed and physically shaking from head to toe – I was practically vibrating. My nerves were completely shot, I slept constantly and felt very low. This was the first time I'd pushed myself way too far. It should've been a lesson – one that I wish I'd accepted. But I'm not great at learning lessons when it comes to my own wellbeing.

It was around this time that I developed a benign tremor in my hands. At first I thought it was down to hunger or too much caffeine, but it never seemed to stop. I can't prove it for certain, but I think I fried my nervous system during that MA period and this was the lasting result. I still have the tremor today – it's something I just live with. Don't ask me to pour you a glass of wine unless you want it in your lap!

In hindsight, I now understand that I was producing too much cortisol and subsequently had a burnout. (Now if that isn't the sexiest phrase you've ever heard, then I don't know what is!) In the same way that adrenalin is released during a period of distress, cortisol levels also rise.

Fawn Hansen talks about adrenal fatigue on her website[1] and references the feeling of being 'wired but tired', which PERFECTLY summarises how I feel during a panic attack, or when I'm very anxious. I couldn't put this into words for so long because I didn't understand it. How could I be 'buzzing' but exhausted at the same time? Well, it's because cortisol burns through the DHEA (didehydroepiandrosterone) hormones in the body. I'll keep the medical stuff brief, but DHEA is the sex hormone. So for women it's oestrogen and for men it's androgens. We need DHEAs to function normally and healthily. It keeps our moods and energy levels steady and our immune system strong. Too much cortisol depletes the DHEA in the same way it does serotonin.

However, one could argue that all this stress eventually paid off because I got my big job in London. I can still recall the conversation with HR. I was in the supermarket buying flowers for my best friend.

Publisher's HR: Hi Claire, I'm just ringing about your interview on Tuesday.

Me: Hello. OK, wonderful. *Thinks, 'Spit it out, woman, this isn't a game show'*

---

1   http://adrenalfatiguesolution.com/what-is-adrenal-fatigue

Publisher's HR: How do you think you did?

Me: *Thinks, 'Just hurry up and tell me!'*
               Erm, I hope I did OK.

Publisher's HR: Well, I'm happy to tell you that we'd
               like to offer you the job.

It's all a bit of a blur after that. I know I tried to hug
the woman behind the pizza deli, but she was having
none of it.

This was the greatest thing that had ever happened
to me (with the exception of discovering dry shampoo).
I had finally achieved something worthwhile, something
that would validate me. Most importantly, this
proved hat I had beaten my anxiety. Surely it would
all go away now that I had achieved my goal? I'd seen
the films: I would move away and become an entirely
new person, a better version of myself. I would buy
a new wardrobe and evolve like a butterfly. I'd be far
away from the troubling experiences of my teenage
years. I could leave it all behind. Running away from
your problems always works, right?

I moved to London four weeks later, into a house
with two other girls. I was OK until my mum gave me
a goodbye hug and then it hit me like a hammer to the
stomach. I had just left home. SHIT. How on earth
was I going to do this on my own?

The new housemates and a bottle of fizz helped
that first night. The girls were very kind to me. But

then how could they avoid the sobbing girl wandering around the house talking to herself: 'Oh my God, what have you done? Are you f**king mental!'

Bolton – population 139,000. London – population 8.5 million. How different could it be really? Well, apart from the transport, pace, people, size and general cost of living, it was all fine. I'll never forget my reaction when I first discovered how much my weekly travel ticket would be (multiple swear words that I won't list).

Still, I was living the dream. I worked in my 'ideal' job for God's sake and the publisher's offices were on The Strand – that's like the red part on the Monopoly board! Talk about high class. Everyone back at home was so proud of me, and despite the shell shock of moving to a new city, I felt excited and alive. As I mentioned in the Introduction, I had a fancy coffee every morning and at one point I even started buying the *Financial Times* (cringe...I couldn't understand a word of it). But I felt good pretending to read it in my lunch hour like a grown up!

The first month of the job flew by. Everyone seemed nice and I could do the work, no problem. As a lover of books I was like a kid in a candy shop! So many new things to read. My direct manager was lovely too, which was a relief. I'd never been around anyone so patient and supportive in the workplace. She also didn't mind my geeky sense of humour, which was a huge bonus. I hadn't really made any friends yet, except for the girl who started at the same time as me, but surely all that would come in time.

Fast forward another five months and things were starting to change. I realised that the office was cliquey and fiercely competitive. At an event one executive drunkenly told me, 'If you want to move up in this place, you need to be loud and make yourself heard.' That seems like a reasonable suggestion. Except, you can't make yourself heard if nobody can see you. The opportunities to mix with higher members of the department or even network were limited for my team. There were no introductions, because...well, networking with us wasn't a priority. We couldn't offer anything in the way of advancement and we didn't work directly with the authors. Which to be fair, I could understand. Everyone's time is limited.

It seemed like the only way to progress was to become an aggressive socialiser. Aggressive as in bold enough to burst into a group full of people and introduce yourself without any fear of rejection. Another way to do this was to attend every event available and be one of the last people standing. Management from certain teams tended to stay late, so this was a good way to make yourself known as a 'fun' person. I managed to do this twice, and on the second occasion I was so drunk that I had a toke on a manager's cigarette. (She didn't even offer it to me, I just reached out thinking it was a really cool thing to do. Plus I don't even smoke!) I might've got away with it if I hadn't burst into a coughing fit.

Straight after this I tried to get a rickshaw driver to take me back to North London. Naturally he refused.

The next day I woke up face down on the stairs, fully clothed with the exception of my shoes, which had somehow ended up in the sink, and wishing I was dead! No amount of bacon and sugary drinks could fix me!

This way of working was foreign to me. Suddenly I couldn't just rely on my brain any more, I had to use my personality. Unfortunately...I HAVE SOCIAL ANXIETY DISORDER and I can't physically stay up until 3am every other night if I have to be in work at 9am. Alcohol affects my serotonin levels (I didn't realise this at the time) and I couldn't do my job properly if I was hungover and feeling on edge.

In typical 'me style' I blamed my lack of networking success all on myself. There was something wrong with me. I was the problem. I was weird, quiet and boring, so of course I wouldn't be accepted into the key social circles. The mental battering from school and university all came flooding back.

The self-analysis started off small. I altered my northern accent to sound more like everyone else and I made an effort to smile constantly. However, within weeks I was replaying conversations in my head from meetings or chance encounters and picking them to pieces. I would replay everything: the dialogue, facial expressions and even tone of voice. Nothing was safe from criticism.

Still, I was determined not to let it stop me. I wouldn't let my anxiety come back again. (Little did I know...it had never left.)

I took a proactive approach. I read lots of books on confidence and how to network (cringe). Surely I could just learn to be like the people around me? I could force it (because that's healthy). First of all, I needed a plan - something to focus on and work towards. I had a keen interest in ebooks and this was the basis of my MA dissertation. So I thought that the digital department would be a great next step.

My view on company progression suddenly changed from being organic to obsessional and I attacked it in the same way I did my degrees. It became all-consuming. I read up on all the latest digital news, revised the jargon and practically memorised the bestselling titles.

One month later I had an opportunity to make myself known to one of the then directors. I'd done my research and approached him at a party. I did my best to appear confident and impress with my knowledge, and I thought it was going well. However, part way through a sentence he bluntly cut me off and said, 'Wow, sexy talk, Claire. I'm guessing you don't have a man in your life.' He then promptly walked off and everyone in the group laughed awkwardly.

Perhaps a tougher person would've brushed off the comment and not taken it personally, but I blushed crimson and sneaked away to the loos to cry a little.

I felt absolutely humiliated. Here was my proof, I really was a freak who didn't belong.

In hindsight, I'd pushed myself too far and had unrealistic expectations. As a result I felt ashamed and ruthlessly criticised myself, rather than feeling pleased by my efforts. I should've felt proud – I'd stepped outside my comfort zone, which was a brave thing to do. But I only felt negative. After this and a few other unfortunate events, I fell into a pit of despair and resentment. I hated everyone around me (again not healthy) and withdrew into myself.

INTERVIEWGATE

I saw an opportunity in another area of the company and applied for the job in the traditional way. To my surprise I was offered an interview! So I did what any obsessional young adult would do. I wrote a list of EVERY question that they could possibly ask and rehearsed the answers like an actor in a play. The final count was 33 questions! Not only was I dealing with the pressure of the interview itself, but with the pressure of learning 33 separate and lengthy answers. If I got a single sentence wrong, I would start again – there was no room for compromise. Looking back now, it makes me shudder. I wasn't being myself, I was forcing myself to be exactly who they wanted me to be. I was a robot trying to attack the task in the same way I had my educational career. Must work harder...must be perfect. In the following days I got up at 5am every morning to practise. **RED FLAG ALERT!**

The night before, I started to notice some very strange and distressing feelings. I'd had palpitations before but this was different. I felt spaced out and floaty, but at the same time my limbs were heavy. Whenever I tried to do some prep, my mouth went dry and my stomach felt knotted. An overwhelming sense of terror and dread began to rise from a deep pit within me, something that I knew I should not have disturbed. I had woken a monster.

After barely five hours sleep, I travelled/staggered into work. As I gripped the seat on the tube I felt a violent contrast between feeling heavy and faint at the same time. I was beginning to get really scared, but I pressed on and forced myself to ignore it. 'You just have to get through the interview.' When I got to work, my stomach (previously in knots) was now quite the opposite. In other words, I thought I might shit myself...not the best way to start the day! I visited the toilets A LOT in the next two hours.

To calm my nerves I decided in all my wisdom to drink a miniature bottle of vodka - seriously, I don't think it can get any more stupid! Unless I decided to do a skydive beforehand or juggle with grenades (I didn't).

When the time came, I made my way towards the HR meeting room. I hope I was walking in a straight line, but who knows? A strange fog spread across my eyes as I moved – it was grey and lights flashed sporadically. At this point most people would probably accept that shit was about to go down, but not me. I like denial land – I'm all about denial land!

I arrived five minutes early and the interviewers were running late (GREAT). So I sat in the room and politely nursed a glass of water (actually, I supped it in two gulps). 'You can do this. Pull yourself together, you'll be fine,' I told myself.

Then IT happened... all so quickly, it happened. Like being tripped up or falling down the stairs, I could see it coming but I was powerless to do anything. I felt a sensation in my head... The only way I can describe it is like a warm wave or current, which I now know was a massive surge of adrenalin. It spread down my arms and across my chest. By the time it reached my heart, everything had 'exploded'. My heart was pounding so hard the sound was deafening. I couldn't catch my breath, my limbs were so heavy I could barely lift them and I was pouring with sweat. I don't think I've ever felt so frightened in my entire life. THIS, ladies and gentlemen, was my first official panic attack. The immediate effect was profound. I didn't care about the interview or even my job any more. I didn't care about anything. All I knew for sure was that I needed to get out of that room NOW.

I opened the glass door with a crash and walked into the HR assistant and the interviewers (who had conveniently chosen this exact moment to turn up). 'I have the norovirus and I must leave at once!', I said. Seriously, I really said it like a Jane Austen character. You can't say that I don't have class, even when I'm shitting myself.

Let's just say that I left the building very quickly after that. (In fact, soon afterwards I left London and went back home to my parents' house. I also cried...A LOT. 'You've finally done it,' I thought, 'you've ruined your life.') There is a lot more detail I could add, but to cut a long story short, by now I was living in a flat with my current and very loving boyfriend, Dan. That evening I ran around the living room sobbing and screaming. I rang NHS Direct to announce that I had 'f**king lost it' and they needed to send an ambulance. They didn't. Craig, the call handler, suggested that I try a warm bath. I then kindly suggested he should 'f**k off and send an ambulance!' They still didn't. I was rolling about on the floor by this point, because it seemed like a good idea. Dan was terrified – poor guy – he'd never seen anything like this. In the end we found a bottle of champagne left over from Christmas (sounds very rock 'n' roll but it wasn't). It was late at night and that was the only alcohol we had in the flat. So I drank an entire bottle of warm bubbly until I fell asleep. Oh, and it all went down on my dad's birthday. I'm nothing if not full on.

GETTING HELP

Once back at my parents' house, I knew that I had to book an appointment with my doctor, but I didn't want to. The idea of trying to articulate what was happening in my brain seemed impossible. I didn't expect to be taken seriously. But after some gentle encouragement from my mum (she made the appointment and dragged me through the door), I did it.

I won't lie and say that it was a wonderful experience (i.e. the doctor stroked my hair and said everything was going to be OK, then tapped her magic wand and I was cured). Actually, it was quite the opposite. She was clinical and almost robotic in her manner. One particularly memorable moment was describing how a panic attack made me feel, whilst sobbing like a child. After a pause, she simply asked, 'Have you tried drinking chamomile tea?' 'ARE YOU F**KING KIDDING ME LADY? I'M PRACTICALLY CLIMBING THE WALLS HERE. I DON'T THINK HERBAL TEA IS THE ANSWER!' I felt like she wasn't 'getting it' at all and I found this very frustrating.

Despite the rough start, it actually turned out to be a life-changing appointment. My doctor signed me off work, prescribed medication and for the first time I had a professional diagnosis to prove that this 'wasn't just in my head', I had a medical condition.

I would like to take this opportunity to defend general practitioners (GPs), even though I've had my fair share of negative experiences. It's easy to label them as being cold and unfeeling. I know I did at first. But, they have on average ten minutes to spend with each patient. It's their job to fix a problem, not provide tea and sympathy (although they may evidently suggest herbal tea). So don't be disheartened if they're not compassionate – it doesn't mean that they don't want to help. Try to think of it this way: mechanics don't give sympathy to a broken car – they just repair it. I definitely think that there is room for improvement in this area, as mental health conditions require a certain level of understanding. A bad experience with medical staff might prevent a person from seeking help in the future.

I remember one incident when I missed a doctor's appointment because my anxiety was high and I couldn't bear the idea of being on public transport. When I rang the surgery, I was told, 'You should really be making more of an effort, Claire, if you want help.' WTF! Are you serious? I left the house twice and had to come back again because I was having panic attacks. 'Make more of an effort?' Can you imagine saying that to a paraplegic? 'Walk to the surgery without a wheelchair or we're not helping you.' Now that's a proper example of 'mental', if you ask me. Still, as much as I would love a doctor to comfort me on an emotional level (and I'm sure there are doctors out there who do provide this for patients), I'd rather they fix the problem.

That evening I decided to type 'social anxiety disorder' into Google (and wait for the word 'freak' to appear on screen). To my surprise a website popped up, one that started me on the path to recovery: Anxiety UK. As I read through the content I was stunned and felt quite emotional. It turns out that I wasn't the only nutter in the world – there's an army of us, a glorious army!

> We can provide support and help if you've been diagnosed with, or suspect you may have an anxiety condition. We can also help you deal with specific phobias such as fear of spiders, blushing, vomiting, being alone, public speaking, heights – in fact, any fear that's stopped you from getting on with your life. (Anxiety UK 2015)

There were people who could actually relate to this kind of thing? I couldn't believe it! It's wonderful that so many mental health charities are now so visible online, but four years ago this was unknown to me. An Anxiety UK call handler was actually the first person I told that I had social anxiety disorder. I burst into tears as soon as I said it, not out of shame (for a change), but because it was a huge relief to finally be honest.

THE RECOVERY

Once I had rested for a good few weeks and taken care of myself, I felt ready to embrace recovery.

Step 1: Come out of the closet

I spent years hiding my condition because I was embarrassed about it. Apologies for repeating myself, but would you be embarrassed if you broke your leg? (I mean, fair enough if it happened in some kind of hardcore sex-play accident.) But really, would you feel embarrassed? I didn't think so. So why is anxiety any different? Easy to say, I know, but I feel the point needs to be made loud and clear. If I broke a bone I'd tell everyone and seek help immediately. Just because you can't see an injury doesn't mean it isn't there.

Being honest about my condition wasn't easy and it certainly didn't come naturally. But it was an important step in my recovery. I felt as though a weight had been lifted from my shoulders. I didn't have to keep this awful secret any more.

So how do you go about 'coming out'? Well, first of all, you need to select your audience. Choose someone whom you trust: your partner, a close friend or a family member. If you don't feel ready to talk to someone you know, why not ring a charity? Anxiety UK, Mind and the Samaritans all provide a confidential phone service. Worried about what to say? Simple: 'I have social anxiety disorder and I just wanted to tell someone.' They'll take it from there.

When telling someone in person, the best advice I can give is to be organised and treat it almost like a mini presentation (the non-scary kind).

✖ Be patient with your audience and remember: they might not understand what you're going through, but they'll listen.

✖ Choose the right time to talk – for example, not during their favourite TV programme or at a party! Car journeys are good for chatting, or even schedule a meeting in the living room. It sounds cheesy, but it's important that you can talk without any distractions.

✖ Tell them how your anxiety makes you feel, both physically and emotionally. You could even list some of the negative thoughts that pop into your head.

✖ Give them the opportunity to ask questions. It's only natural to be curious.

Step 2: Being honest at work

✖ Telling your employer is desirable, but not always a good idea and should be played by ear. If you can't tell a senior member of the team, then maybe confide in a colleague that you're close to. It's good to have someone 'who knows' at work.

✖ If you plan on talking to your manager, you might want to give them a 'heads up' via email.

✖ If you've started a new job, don't mention your condition until your probation period is over (just to be on the safe side). I hope this won't be necessary but after probation you're entitled to more employment rights.

✖ Anxiety is a registered mental illness and must be taken seriously under the Equality Act 2010.[2] However, if you don't feel as though you can talk to your manager, then schedule a meeting with HR – part of their responsibility is employee wellbeing.

✖ Prepare a speech beforehand so that you're clear about what you're going to say. Assure them that it won't affect your performance, but liken it to a virus that might require patience at times. Also encourage them to ask questions.

✖ Remember, you can only be absent from work without a sick note for a certain number of working days (seven in the UK).

✖ Discrimination is real – contact the Time to Change[3] team if you would like to discuss an incident.

---

2 For further information, visit www.gov.uk/guidance/equality-act-2010-guidance

3 Time to Change is a charity dedicated to ending the stigma and discrimination experienced by people with mental health problems. For more information, visit www.time-to-change.org.uk

You don't have to be ashamed of who you are (unless of course you're Hitler – he can f**k right off).

Step 3: Moving forward and listening to your body

I only had a month off work, but it felt like an age and coming back was nerve-wracking. But I was overwhelmed by the amount of support I received, particularly from my manager. We began to have weekly catch-ups to see how I was doing.

I had to accept that my career would need to take a back seat until my health improved. There was no need to rush. My body had taken a battering during the last year and it might be a while until I was back at full strength again. It took me around nine months in total, which might seem like a long time, but I wanted to really do things right.

When it comes to careers, ultimately I think it's great to have a goal, but be careful that it doesn't become an all-consuming obsession. Remember, the brain can only cope with so much before a burnout. After my breakdown, I finally learned this important lesson. I also realised that despite external pressures and worries you CAN make it your way and by being yourself. In time I did progress and I did it on my own terms.

Chapter 5

OUT AND ABOUT IN PUBLIC

In this chapter I'm going to discuss what lies at the heart of social anxiety: SOCIAL SITUATIONS! These are the very events and interactions that make us feel so uncomfortable. Social anxiety is the ultimate fun sucker – it takes something that should be pleasant and distorts it. But it really doesn't have to be this way. By following or adapting the strategies and exercises in this chapter, you can combat the anxiety and not only embrace social situations but enjoy them too. Life is too short to be a slave to fear.

THE PARTY CRASHER

'I'm having a party this weekend, you should come': a phrase guaranteed to strike fear into the heart of all social anxiety sufferers. Others include: 'Are you coming for drinks after work?' or 'Can you attend the event tonight?' A feeling of dread is closely followed by butterflies/hungry piranhas in the stomach. Negative thought cycles begin to form. They look something like this:

'Oh God I don't want to go. How can I get out of this?'

'No, I really should go. I'll get a reputation for being boring or a flake.'

'But what if it's awful and I can't think of anything to talk about?'

'No, I'm being ridiculous – it'll be fine.'

'Oh God, I don't want to go.'

'Well, you should!'

'But I can't!'

It becomes an argument between two sides of the brain.

Just to clarify the situation right now: I am NOT a recluse! Social anxiety can be mistaken for being 'a miserable cow', or a hermit. Someone who likes to binge-watch TV in the dark, drinking wine. (For the record, I only do that on Tuesday nights and I LOVE it!) I really enjoy spending time with others and being sociable, but in the past my anxiety has crippled my ability to do so.

The negative thought cycle is no stranger to me. As I mentioned previously, it's been with me since I was a child. Every few months there would be a family gathering of some sort. BBQs, birthdays... Somebody was always bloody doing something! For me, the worst part was the drive over there. I would feel sick with nerves and dread the initial five minutes, filled with awkward embraces and greeting family friends whom I hadn't seen in years. I felt an expectation to 'perform' in front of the other adults and I didn't want to disappoint my parents (not that they put any pressure on me). Normal children chat animatedly about school and they play with the other children outside. They do cartwheels in the living room and eat too much food. I tried my best as I didn't want to be labelled as strange. But somehow the words 'quiet' and 'shy' were used in reference to me. That's the frustrating thing about being a child: adults talk about you as though you can't hear them! 'You remember Claire, don't you, Sandra? She's very shy. Say "hello", Claire.' Suddenly, all the eyes in the room would dart in my direction, seeking a peek at the 'shy girl', the one who isn't normal. Or at least that's how I felt.

When I was 13, a friend invited me to her birthday slumber party. It was my first-ever sleepover and while I was excited, I was also really nervous. I didn't know all of the girls that well and we'd be sleeping in the same room. What if I embarrassed myself by snoring or talking in my sleep? Or worse still, what if they played some horrible practical joke on me? I'd seen that type of thing in American teen movies. They'd tell everyone at school and I'd become a laughing stock. I'd probably be an outcast and end up alone in the gutter (my negative thinking started at a young age).

So I came up with the ultimate back-up plan, just in case. I would hide in the toilets and play games on my phone. There were eight girls at the party – surely I wouldn't be missed and, besides, I was sure that nobody would need to use the toilet at any point. It was foolproof! The evening started out well enough – we watched a movie, painted our nails and ate lots of junk food. Then suddenly out of nowhere it was decided that we would play 'Truth or Dare' (shit). Now was the time to activate my plan! So I crept away to my secret hiding place. Everything was going to be just fine. Unfortunately, after half an hour somebody did come to find me. Bollocks! There I was, minding my own business, playing a game, when there was a knock at the door.

Friend 1:	Claire? Are you in there?
Me:	*Five seconds of panicked silence* Erm, yeah. I'm here.
Friend 2:	*Loud whisper* Is she in there? What's she doing?
Me:	*Thinks, 'OMG all of you just f**k off!'*

Friend 1:   Are you OK? You've been ages.

Me: *More panicked silence* No...erm, I think I'm locked in.

Friend 1:   Why didn't you say anything?

Me: *Thinks, 'Please let me die now!'* I've been shouting for ages. Didn't you hear me?

That's right, people... The only plausible solution I could think of was to pretend that I was locked in. It was either that or tell them I was constipated, and that was not going to happen! So I rattled the door handle theatrically to make it look more legit. I was a damsel in distress, not some weirdo who hides in the toilet. Everything would be fine right?

Fast forward an hour later and the girl's dad had to break the door down. Oops. In hindsight I feel like I really should've just played Truth or Dare. It's a bitch, huh.

Despite this disastrous first attempt, it wouldn't be the last time I executed this plan. The only difference is that I upgraded to public toilets (more cubicles to hide in). If worst comes to worst, I can just pretend that I feel sick, right?

Make it through the party and have fun

Despite the nerves that they induce, parties and social occasions are intended to be fun rather than torturous! Your anxiety may try to distort this, but do your best to keep an open mind. I once walked out of a party because somebody mentioned board games. Again, I say 'walked' but it was definitely a run (I used the norovirus excuse again). I imagined getting every question wrong and looking like an idiot, which is a real shame because the party sounded like fun afterwards and I bloody love board games!

TIPS: Here are my suggestions for ways to prepare yourself for social occasions:

✖ It's useful to remember that the event is always worse in your head than in reality (you'd be surprised how we work ourselves up). In my experience, the first five minutes are awkward and weird, but then you settle into your surroundings and it gets easier. So it's comforting to remember the following statement before turning up: 'The way I'm feeling now is the worst I will feel – it can only get better from here.'

✖ Decide what you're going to wear at least two days in advance. This sounds obvious, but having one less thing to worry about on the night will help. Choose something simple, comfortable, but also something that makes you feel good.

✖ For the love of God, please don't try a new make-up look or hairstyle before an event (we've all done it). There's a 90 per cent chance that it'll go wrong and this will only add to your stress levels. It's hard enough going to an event if you're anxious, let alone worrying that you look like a drag act!

✖ Be honest and tell one other person how you're feeling. You don't have to make it 'a thing' – just say, 'I'm feeling a bit nervous about tonight. I'm sure I'll be fine but I just wanted you to be aware in case I need a minute to decompress.' This will take some of the pressure away.

✖ Get yourself a drink – they don't call it 'Dutch courage' for nothing! I'm not suggesting that alcohol is a long-term solution and it shouldn't be used as a crutch, but let's be honest: it usually takes the edge of nerves. (One drink, NOT five. You don't want to be that stupid cow who got so drunk she fell into a bush!) Often alcohol has a placebo effect, so in time one hopes you won't need it any more.

✖ Practise in the mirror. I know that sounds weird, but hear me out. Sometimes I practise saying phrases in the mirror with a smile. It'll feel strange at first, but it really helps.

✖ Say positive affirmations to yourself two minutes before you enter the venue. Phrases such as 'You are f**king awesome!' and 'Oh my God, you are the coolest person here.' Say them loudly (in your head). This will flood the brain with happy endorphins and help balance out the nerves. It's only a temporary boost, but it will get you through the door.

✖ Do a CBT thought chart exercise (see Chapter 2) in advance.

✖ If a panic attack happens, take a moment and let it run. Remember the exposure therapy exercise in Chapter 2. Having an attack is a good thing because it enables you to practise with the sensation. It's just a nasty trick, not a prediction of bad things to come.

PERSONAL APPEARANCE

If you have social anxiety, then the chances are that you struggle with your appearance. Feeling insecure about the way one looks isn't unique to anxiety. It starts at puberty for most teenagers. I've already mentioned that I wanted to be blonde, tanned and have big boobs from ages 12–17. (Seriously, it was bad. The smell of my fake tan cream is forever etched into my brain.) Then came my Goth phase – such a cliché, I know.

I also had flare-ups of acne that lasted well into my mid-20s. I'm talking about painful cysts that permanently used to reside around my chin. I was very insecure about my face, but on the plus side it did help me to develop some excellent make-up skills at a young age. A few quick tips if you have acne:

✖ Go and visit your doctor if the condition is new to you as it may be hormonal.

✖ Drink shed-loads of water. It will help to flush your pores out from the inside.

✖ Eat lots of salmon and take Omega 3 supplements.

✖ Have a look at beauty blog Caroline Hirons' website.[1] Her advice is golden!

✖ Don't use toothpaste on spots – it's an old wives' tale. It will only dry out the skin, not the spot.

✖ Use products with salicylic acid in them. Acid makes it sound scary, but it isn't. Salicylic kills spots without leaving scars.

✖ Avoid sugar. A sugar spike will cause the body to create sebum. An influx of sebum causes spots.

---

1   www.carolinehirons.com/2012/05/acne-cheat-sheet.html

✖ Most importantly, do not try to burst/squeeze/ destroy cysts (these are the lumps under your skin). It took me five years to finally accept that you will never win this fight. Believe me, I know how strong the urge to get rid of them is, but agitating them won't help. All you will do is cause scarring and spread the bacteria. The best thing to do is to leave them be and use a salicylic acid product.

I think everyone feels insecure about their appearance from time to time, but the important thing to remember is perspective. I didn't just feel slightly insecure – in contrast, I was certain that I was an ugly duckling and I obsessed about it. At one point, I went to the toilets every ten minutes to check that my fringe looked a certain way. People used to tease me for being 'vain'. They had no idea! My parents and friends could never understand it. 'You're such a beautiful girl, Claire,' my mum would say. If only that helped, but it just doesn't right? You can't believe them.

At the risk of sounding like a boring sod, I'll say it does get easier the older you get – mainly because you start to give less of a shit and your brain is naturally focused on other things.

Ultimately, there are ways to tackle anxiety about personal appearance. Nobody should have to feel ugly. Work through it in stages as this will build stronger foundations. Walking around repeating affirmations such as 'I am a Goddess' didn't do it for me.

CBT exercises can be very effective (see Chapter 2). Do you have any solid evidence that you could present to a judge that proves you're ugly? How many people have actually told you out loud that you're ugly/fat/have big ears? (Cruel sibling taunts don't count.)

It took me a long time to finally accept that I couldn't control everything about my appearance. I wanted blonde hair; it was brown. I wanted green eyes; they were blue. I wanted curves; I was stick thin.

I still have 'ugly' days when I feel bad about myself and have a desire to hide from the world. But it's normal and as much as I'd like to feel super-confident every day, I accept that this isn't achievable and that's OK!

TIPS

✖ Number one rule: when you're feeling vulnerable DO NOT look at fashion magazines. Torturing yourself with 'perfect' airbrushed photos of people who don't actually exist won't help.

✖ Ration the mirror! If you're a mirror addict like me, be strict and only allow yourself one look an hour. Looking more won't make you feel better.

DATING

Dating can be tricky if you have social anxiety...meeting someone new, talking about yourself, intense eye contact. I feel nervous just thinking about it! Let's be honest, a first date is basically an interview but with alcohol. And there is *sooooo* much to analyse afterwards. This is a situation in which, without a shadow of a doubt, you ARE being judged and evaluated. Afterwards I would replay each conversation in my mind. It's not just the meeting-up aspect of dating that I struggle with, either. Texting/Whatsapping – let's talk about that nasty pitfall. Tell me, how does a text have the power to alter your mood for the entire day? It doesn't matter whether you've passed your exams, got a new job or found a cure for cancer, a disappointing text from someone you 'like' can make everything else feel like shit. Below is an example text conversation from a guy I dated briefly years ago. Bear in mind that it took me around 30 minutes to think of something really witty, cool but flirty to say.

Me: Afternoon stranger! Guess who? It was a surprise to bump into you last night. [Not a surprise at all – I'd worn my best dress and new shoes, and checked his Facebook in advance to make sure that he'd be at that particular bar.] We should meet one night this week if you're around?

Him: [Two HOURS later] Dunno, I'm skint right now LOL.

IS THAT ALL I FREAKING GET? SERIOUSLY... DID YOU SEE MY AMAZING TEXT? IT WAS PRACTICALLY A LITERARY SENSATION AND HE COULDN'T EVEN BE BOTHERED TO WRITE THE WORDS 'I DON'T KNOW' PROPERLY.

I spent all afternoon waiting in agony for the text to arrive and then all evening obsessing about what it meant. Deep down, I knew he wasn't 'that into me', but I couldn't stop myself. (What did I tell you? The mammalian is the strongest part of the brain.)

> **TIP:** If you're prone to obsessing about messages, simplify the situation and give your phone to a friend. It removes the temptation and you'll feel better for it, trust me. I had a bad habit of texting people when drunk, so after 9pm on nights out my best mate would automatically confiscate my phone, just in case.

After a month of living in London, my housemate decided that I needed to meet some new people and she convinced me to join a dating site. Now, from my limited experience I thought that dating websites were used by perverts and paedophiles. But after a glass of wine I was willing to give it a go.

Amazingly this is how I met my boyfriend, Dan. I'll never forget our first date. I couldn't believe that I was meeting someone whom I didn't know. He could be a murderer! Travelling to Camden on the tube, I keenly checked my face and hair for any flaw. Being a perfectionist also extends to my appearance and I can always find fault.

The first thing I ever said to him was 'Well, this is weird.' Talk about a good first impression – I just blurted it out. In fairness though, he went in for a hug and I'm more of a handshake person. So we both committed faux pas.

My physical symptoms were playing up big time – blushing and tremors in particular. My hands were shaking so bad that I had to sit on them! He was asking me lots of questions and I wanted to scream, 'Stop looking at me for five seconds, will you!' If I could just have a few sips of my wine, then I knew everything would calm down. But he wouldn't avert his attention! Fortunately, he bent down to tie his shoe lace, in which time I saw my chance and consumed half the glass in a few gulps!

When I officially started dating Dan, everything felt fresh and new. Just as I tried to reinvent myself at work, I wanted to make the right impression in my personal life. I was a fun and relaxed individual, not some nutter who hid in toilets!

We were wandering around central London one afternoon and everything was rosy, when suddenly he said, 'My friends are in a pub nearby. Would you like to come and meet them?' I can summarise my internal reaction in one word: 'ARRRRRRRRRRRGGGGGGGGGHHHH!'

My hair looked a mess, I wasn't wearing the right outfit and I hadn't had an alcoholic beverage. Never mind world poverty, THIS right here was a complete nightmare. 'Of course, that's sounds great. I'd love to!' I said in the chirpiest, most non-freaked-out voice I could manage. We'd only been together for three months and I didn't want him to see the crazy just yet. After ten minutes we arrived at the pub.

Dan: I think they're at the back.

Me: Do you want a drink? I'll get us one.

Dan: Yeah, in a minute though. Let's go over and say 'hi' first.

Me: Oh, it's no trouble. You go over and I'll join you in a minute.

Dan: No, let's go over together.

Me: *Thinks 'Let me go to the bar, you motherf**ker. I need to down a glass of wine!'*

Dan: You OK?

Me: Of course! *Said a little too enthusiastically*
                 Let's go over then.

As we walked towards the group, I gripped his hand tightly. I needed to make a good impression and I was going to fail miserably. I could feel myself blushing as he introduced me. Why was I such a freak? Everybody was nice enough and fortunately had been drinking most of the afternoon, so I don't think they noticed my awkwardness too much...or the fact that I was grinning like a Cheshire Cat on acid.

   After 20 minutes he turned to me.

Dan: I'm just nipping to the loo. Everything
                 OK?

Claire: Yeah, sure, I'll be fine. *Thinks 'I will
                 f**king rip your throat out if you leave
                 me here with all these strangers'*

The things we do for love, huh?

   A few months later on our first holiday, I locked myself in the bathroom, sobbing because I couldn't hide my demons any longer. The anxiety came bursting through as it always does. Fortunately, he still loved me, bathroom madness and all. But I wouldn't recommend telling a partner in such a dramatic way!

   Five years later and we're still together. I'm a very lucky lady.

TIPS

✖ Text a friend beforehand and be honest about how you're feeling. (You'll notice this advice popping up time and again because it's an important one for me.) Being honest will take some of the sting out of the situation. I would normally text a friend and say, 'I'm feeling really nervous about this date. Please can you text me some amazing things about myself?'

✖ Be the first to arrive. Not by an hour – ten minutes should suffice. There's nothing more awkward than having someone watch you arrive. Plus, you can use the time to decompress and get comfy in your surroundings. Plus, if you've suffered any wardrobe malfunctions you can sort this – it's important to feel as comfortable as possible. Before my date with Dan, you could practically see your reflection in my nose, it was so shiny. (In my defence, it was summer and I'd just been on a boiling hot train.) In that situation, arriving early allowed me to cover my face with enough powder to sink a ship! When your date arrives, act like you only just got there (obviously).

✖ Jot down topics in advance that you can discuss. Films, job roles, etc. (Put them in your phone. You can always pretend to be checking a text.)

✖ Try not to get too 'hyped up' about the whole thing (easier said than done, I know). You're just meeting another person and if it all goes tits up then so be it. It's not the end of the world. If you do find yourself getting worked up, that's OK – just do some distraction techniques to engage the brain. (See also Chapter 2.)

✖ Do a CBT thought chart exercise (see Chapter 2) in advance to rationalise any negative thoughts.

PUBLIC TRANSPORT

Now for a quick note on public transport during rush hour: it's SHIT. There's no other way to describe it, really. Most people with anxiety find it difficult to endure and I'm no exception.

Imagine this scene – It's 8:15am and, as usual, you leave the house to travel to your place of work. As you approach your local train station, you notice that the platforms are already swarming with bodies. But you have no choice but to join them as you need to get to work. As the train arrives, agitated people start to jostle with one another, trying to force their way to the front. The doors open and the current passengers practically spill out of the carriage because it's so full. Those standing next to you moan loudly, 'Oh for God's sake', then decide to push their way onto the train, and you're caught in the current. Suddenly you find yourself pressed against multiple strangers without a centimetre of space between you. You're trapped and there's nothing to hold onto. The train sets off with a jolt. It's too hot, the man standing to your left is wearing a rucksack that pokes into your chest, and in the corner a small child is screaming. 'It's OK,' you tell yourself, 'it'll be over soon.' The train pulls into the next stop and, to your horror, more people push their way on. You are now being crushed. Your face is smothered in another woman's hair and you're finding it hard to stay upright. You can't breathe properly and begin to panic, your eyes frantically darting from left to right, looking for escape. 'I'm going to faint. If I fall, I'll be trampled. I need to get off.' After another agonising ten minutes, the train pulls into a popular station and your fellow commuters flood out from the carriages, with you caught in the wave. With shaking limbs you sit on the platform and burst into tears.

This isn't your stop, but you can't bring yourself to get back on the train.

This was me, the day I was late for work. When I eventually made it, a colleague asked about my tear-stained face. While she was sympathetic, she also said, 'Well, nobody likes rush hour. We all just have to get on with it.' I completely agree with the sentiment: nobody likes to be squashed against other commuters like cattle. It's a highly unpleasant experience, one that turns normally rational and polite people into raging bulls. It isn't an acceptable way for anyone to travel, and I don't believe that I am deserving of special treatment or consideration any more than the next person.

However, the lack of understanding of the difficulties that those with mental health conditions experience on public transport is alarming. If I was in a wheelchair, suddenly people would understand (as they should), but having a panic attack and crying merely makes a person 'dramatic' and 'fragile'. The colleague later said with a grin, 'You need to toughen up a bit.' I accepted it at the time, but now I find it infuriating.

TIPS: We can't expect miracles changes to be made to transport, so in the meantime here are a few suggestions:

✖ Make sure that you've eaten and had something to drink before travelling. While panic attacks don't cause fainting, low blood sugar can do! (I found this out the hard way and my boyfriend had to drag me off the train.)

✖ Always carry a bottle of water.

✖ Create a relaxing playlist or listen to an audio book to distract your brain.

✖ If you find yourself starting to panic, do some belly breathing (see Chapter 2). This will increase the amount of oxygen in the body.

✖ If the train is too crowded and you don't feel comfortable, DON'T get on. Being late for work isn't a good enough reason to sacrifice your wellbeing.

✖ If you're really struggling, talk to your employer and enquire if you can work from home a few days a week.

✖ It isn't ideal, but travelling earlier (as I do) is a good way to avoid overcrowding. You can use the time to exercise, read or have a leisurely breakfast.

WORK IT

Work events tended to be the ones that I found the most difficult. They almost felt like live theatre, an occasion to perform and impress. Definitely not the time to 'be myself'. So I used to mimic body language, accent and even tone of voice to match the others. At one point I even caught myself posing – it was exhausting. Mass social interaction is not something that comes naturally to me. It's something that I've learned over time and I've trained myself how to act with confidence.

At a book launch I was asked to 'look after' two buyers from a popular supermarket. This commenced 45 minutes of excruciating dialogue and awkward silences. They were clearly only there for the free booze (fair enough) and to meet the celebrity author. It was like playing a game of 20 Questions – only 'yes' or 'no' responses were given.

Me: Are you enjoying the evening?

Buyer 1:   Yes.

Me: Have you travelled far?

Buyer 2:   Yes.

Me: Can I get either of you a drink?

Buyer 1:   No.

Me: Oh, are you the one driving then?! [My attempt at a joke]

Buyer 1 and 2: *Silence*

Me: It's such a great book. Have you had chance to flick through it?

Buyer 2:   No.

Buyer 1:   When are we going to meet [Celebrity Author]?

Me: *Thinks, 'Only after I shove my heel up your arse!'*

Without a doubt, the hardest part of any work event is the arrival: walking into a sea of bodies and noise, desperately searching for a familiar face. Who am I going to talk to? Where should I stand? What am I going to talk about?

I've learned a few survival tips during my four years in the big city. The first thing to remember is that feeling nervous is a completely *normal* reaction – it doesn't make you a freak or a loser. Whenever you enter a work event, at least 50 per cent of the people in the room will have similar concerns to yours. They might hide it behind loud voices and big smiles, but at the end of the day everybody likes to feel accepted – we're human, after all!

TIPS

✖ Don't be late. Rushing only increases the heart rate and will leave you feeling flustered. Preferably arrive with enough time to freshen up in the toilets and acclimatise to the surroundings before entering. Comfort goes a long way in situations like these. I like to make sure that I'm not carrying heavy bags or feeling sweaty.

✖ If you are late, don't burst into the room. Take two minutes to breathe and allow your heart rate to stabilise.

✖ Body language is important. Amy Cuddy, a researcher at Harvard University, talks about the importance of power poses (Hochman 2014). If you adopt a high power pose before entering a situation that makes you nervous, it can help you to feel more confident. When I first read about power poses, I thought it was a barmy idea. How could standing a certain way improve my confidence? But after trying them out I'm now a convert! These poses have a positive impact on hormones in the body. Try them for a few minutes before you attend an event! (I would, however, advise that you do this in private.)

Power poses

✖ Remember the CBT thought chart exercise in Chapter 2. Challenge any negative thoughts in advance.

✖ If you find small talk a challenge, jot down a few topics in advance – there's no shame in it. Good ones are: Have you travelled far? What department do you work in? How do you know so and so? Are you doing anything nice this weekend? They might sound lame, but they're easy and are guaranteed to start a conversation.

✖ Don't fight your emotions. If something bad happens, such as a rebuff from a colleague or mild embarrassment, simply take yourself away to the loos for five minutes (remember, they're a haven) and allow yourself to feel whatever you're feeling – don't suppress it. Remind yourself that you're human and you're doing just fine. Then feel pleased that you made the effort and leave the toilets with your head held high. In an hour it won't even matter any more. Embrace the feeling, accept it, feel it, rationalise it, disregard it, move forward. Don't carry negative thoughts and feelings around with you all evening – it's best to let them have centre stage for a short period of time and then brush them aside. If all else fails, then just have a few glasses of wine and put it down to experience! You should feel proud that you stepped outside of your comfort zone.

✖ We spend the majority of our time focusing on what we can't control rather than what we can. For example, you can't control what people think of you. Professor X can, but you can't. However, you can control how you treat yourself.

✖ Go for the safer targets! Start small, don't go and talk to the MD at your first attempt! Look for someone on their own or a small group at the edge of the room. Chances are they'll be feeling awkward too and will happily receive your attention.

✖ Don't stay with your pack. Try to resist the temptation to stick with your close colleagues. Encourage yourself to talk to one new person. In my experience it's easier to network on your own than in a group, as you push yourself that bit more. If you can do this, or at least try, it will make you feel calmer when attending the next event because you'll know that you can do it. Also, if your pack spreads out, it'll be easier for each of you to join other groups later on (as you can introduce each other).

PUBLIC SPEAKING

Allow me to crowbar in a little section on public speaking, because if you have social anxiety, it's the ultimate worst nightmare! For me, public speaking isn't just defined by being on stage in front of an audience – it can also mean speaking in a meeting, or re-telling an anecdote to people at a dinner party. Basically, it's anything that involves being observed. For some people it comes naturally and for others it doesn't and that's OK! However, it is a skill that can be acquired if you want to learn how.

When I was in the early recovery stages from my nervous breakdown I could barely sit in a meeting room, let alone participate. It's important – and I can't stress this enough – to be stable before you attempt to build your confidence around public speaking.

TIPS

✖ Practise beforehand. Even if you just have to say a few words in a meeting, practise what you're going to say (preferably in front of a mirror). This will allow your brain to become more familiar with the idea and you'll get used to hearing your voice out loud and in a formal situation. Surprisingly, that can be a shock to most people.

✖ If you suffer badly with physical symptoms such as blushing or shaking, you might want to talk to your doctor about propranolol (a beta blocker). As I mentioned in Chapter 2, this medication will help. I don't want to sound like a drug pusher, but I do speak the truth. The effects are fairly instantaneous – when necessary, I take a tablet 15 minutes beforehand.

✖ A sports psychologist once told me, 'Try and imagine that the butterflies in your stomach are actually sparks of excitement. Imagine that you're going to do an amazing job and you can't wait to get in there!' This sounds a bit farfetched, but I've experienced really good results from. Say to yourself (mentally), 'I'm going to be fantastic. I cannot wait to show everyone how great I am.' Smile as you're saying/thinking it.

✖ Be sure to adopt the 'power poses' beforehand to give yourself a boost.

At the end of the day, if it all goes tits up then that's OK. It might not feel like it, but it doesn't matter. Next time will be better – remember that. You should feel proud that you tried.

Below is a list of public-speaking-related events that I have done in the last three years. I haven't included these in order to brag, but purely to make the point that public speaking is a skill that can be learned, even if you have social anxiety. Please also bear in mind that when I was first signed off work by a doctor I could barely leave the house!

✖ Stood up and played charades in front of 15 people.

✖ Led meetings by myself.

✖ Went on the radio.

✖ Was interviewed for a documentary.

- ✖ Gave two work-related presentations in front of 100 people.

- ✖ Gave a 20-minute talk at a charity event for The Samaritans.

It took a while and lots of practice, but I got there.

Remember to be kind to yourself. People with mental health conditions are the worst culprits for berating themselves and belittling any successes. For example, 'Why should I feel proud that I spoke in that meeting? I mean, I should be able to do that naturally, right? I shouldn't feel pleased with myself – if anything, that just highlights how weak I am.' I can't imagine anyone saying to Andy Murray after he scores the winning point, 'Oh, [big whoop] you hit the ball over the net.'

It's as simple as this: if you find something difficult and you do it anyway (whether it turns out the way you want or not), this is a success. You've taken steps to improve your anxiety and that is fantastic! Therefore, I would like you to avoid using the following phrases:

'It was nothing.'

'It was only this.'

'I should be able to do it anyway.'

Instead feel proud and reward yourself. A reward can be anything from a chocolate bar, a bottle of champagne or a car (if you're made of money). Just something that communicates to your brain that you did a good thing.

PLEASING OTHER PEOPLE

Wanting to have the support of your family, friends and peers is a relatively innate thing. Nobody likes to feel rejected. However, it's important that your own happiness and peace of mind are not determined by the mood and approval of others. I like to please others and always have done. In theory this sounds like a lovely idea, but in reality, it's draining and completely unattainable.

There are always going to be people in life who make us feel more anxious than others and no amount of 'pleasing' will improve the situation. I dread organising social events with certain people, because I know I'll do something wrong. It's inevitable. I'll pick the wrong restaurant or an inconvenient time, or the seats won't be right and we'll have to move. I spend the whole evening on edge, trying desperately to keep them entertained. By the end of the night I'm exhausted and need half of the following day to recover. I very much doubt that these people realise how much it affects me and to a certain extent it's my fault because I allow myself to get worked up.

The older I get, the more I realise that disagreements aren't pleasant, but they're natural and shouldn't be blown out of proportion. Don't be so afraid to say the 'wrong' thing. Everybody has the right to be assertive. If an angry exchange of words does follow, try not to panic. It could partially be down to shock (on the other person's part). They're not used to being disagreed with and are reacting from a place of emotion. On the other hand, they could simply believe they're right and want to further argue the point. As long as their responses aren't personal (e.g. 'You're a moron!'), then this is fine.

Things are easier said than done – being honest and expressing your opinion can be nerve-wracking, especially if you don't like conflict. Like many things, it takes practice. Obviously, don't say something just for the sake of it. It needs to be relevant. First of all, take a deep breath and if you really can't continue the conversation, ask for a moment to think. Here's an example. Whenever I meet up with a friend of mine, she tends to choose a time and location that suits her best. Not wanting to rock the boat I used to agree, even though it was inconvenient. One day I decided to be more assertive. I was terrified that she might be angry and refuse to meet me, but I needed to try this.

Friend: You still up for having drinks tomorrow? I was thinking we could go to that retro bar and have cocktails. [Basically, a ten-minute walk from where she lives and a lengthy train journey for me]

Me: Actually, that's quite far for me to travel. I thought we could meet somewhere halfway?

Friend: *Pause* Erm...it's been a busy week and
                I'm tired. I'd rather go somewhere local.
                Would you mind?

Me: *Deep breath* You poor thing, I hope you
                have a relaxing weekend planned? The
                thing is, I'm rather tired myself, but I'd
                really like to catch up. There must be a
                place that's easy for us both to get to.

Friend: I might have to give it a miss then. It's
                been a hell of a week.

Me: OK, no problem. Rest up this weekend.

That might sound like a failure, but it's actually a
success. In the past I would've travelled for an hour and
spent the first part of the evening feeling frustrated.
Why did she always get her own way? Well the truth
is, because I let her. She wasn't a malicious person – in
fact, she was and still is a great friend. She was just
used to me doing whatever she wanted.

I was shaking as I put the phone down and all types
of worries raced through my mind. 'What if she never
spoke to me again? Should I have just agreed to meet
her?' But again I took a deep breath, went back to my
desk and carried on with my work. An hour later she
rang back, apologised and agreed to meet me halfway.

The hardest part is taking the first step.

TIPS: Come up with some key phrases and say them out loud. I do this in front of the mirror. You feel ridiculous at first, but it's a great way to practise.

✖ Actually I'd rather not have sushi for lunch. Can we try somewhere else?

✖ It would be great if you could pick me up – I think I'll struggle on the bus.

✖ Please don't call me an idiot as it really hurts my feelings.

✖ I'm sorry but I can't meet up today as I'm tired after a long day at work.

They all seem quite trivial, but it's a good place to start. It's a case of experiencing the discomfort that comes when disagreeing with someone and building on it.

A few dos and don'ts:

✖ DO pick your battles. Only choose examples that genuinely bother you. Don't have a discussion just for the sake of it.

✖ DON'T be aggressive. As soon as you lash out at someone with angry words, you've lost. It's better to keep things non-personal and focused on the discussion at hand. For example, rather than saying, 'You always make me come to you – you're so selfish,' try 'I'd really like it if we could meet halfway.'

✖ DON'T over-explain your position. If you decline an invitation and the person asks what you're doing instead, be polite but brief. There is no need to explain your decision (unless you're missing their birthday!).

✖ DO complete a CBT thought chart (see Chapter 2) before an encounter that makes you feel really anxious. It's good to neutralise any negative thoughts.

✖ DON'T cave in to peer pressure. A colleague once tried to make me come out with her by repeatedly calling me 'boring' in front of the team. It was harmless enough, but it made me feel exposed. Despite her relentless tactics, I simply smiled and declined the invitation once more, suggesting that I would come another time.

Chapter 6

THE TIGER, THE BULLY AND THE FRENEMY

Anxiety is the master of keeping us trapped. It's a crafty sod that can, and does, take on many forms, like a shape shifter. Remember that its overall goal is always the same: to keep you trapped and stuck in a routine. Over time I've identified the main three characters to watch out for, and some handy tips for dealing with them:

THE TIGER

This character is impossible to ignore. He (apologies – I just see him as male) triggers very aggressive physical symptoms and distressing thoughts, such as 'STOP, you can't do this. Leave now!' He often appears right before a stressful event. You'll feel him sink his claws in like a dead weight on your back as he demands attention. The Tiger also appears at night time. He is an enforcer of insomnia: 'You won't sleep. You're going to be tired again tomorrow, you can't cope with anything!'

Treatment: Belly breathing exercises (see Chapter 2). Acknowledge and accept the attack (the Tiger). Don't fight it; allow yourself to feel afraid. Keep moving. Follow the steps from exposure therapy (again, see Chapter 2).

THE BULLY

This character is cruel and belittling and mainly exploits the emotional symptoms of insecurity and self-doubt. 'You're pathetic. Who would want to speak to you? You're going to embarrass yourself. You're a failure.' Does that sound familiar? It's the Bully talking.

Treatment: Don't argue, as you won't win. Instead, do a CBT thought chart or/and a positive refocus exercise (see Chapter 2). Take a moment to do this properly and really drag all of those negative thoughts to the surface. Embrace them, allow yourself to feel bad for a moment, rationalise them and then keep moving.

THE FRENEMY

This is the sneakiest character of all and I visualise her as female. She convinces you that 'doing nothing' is actually the right decision. There are no physical symptoms and no cruel trash talk. Instead she strikes with kindness. This is the character that I would really like to focus on, because she often goes undetected. I was recently talking to a friend of mine who's been having trouble with anxiety for years. Her 'go to' response is to avoid situations that make her feel anxious, and the tragic part is, she doesn't even realise she's doing it.

Friend: I've been thinking about Adam's party and I've decided to give it a miss. I've been doing so much lately. I'm really tired and probably a bit hormonal. I'm just going to have a relaxing night in and watch TV. I'm sure everyone will understand.

Me: *Thinks, 'Noooooo...do you know how many times I've heard you say this? You're being tricked into maintaining your anxiety. It might feel uncomfortable at first, but you can do this'*

Now don't get me wrong, I'm a big believer in relaxation. I think that sleep and 'down time' are very important, particularly if you struggle with mental illness. However, they can also be used as an excuse to 'check out' of life and avoid dealing with problems. The Frenemy tricks a person into believing that if they 'just relax and give the party/meeting/holiday a miss', they'll feel better. The truth is, that's rarely the case. Believe me, I wish it was because I would've been cured years ago! In contrast, you're being fooled into hiding from situations that make you nervous, thereby strengthening any anxious beliefs.

From experience, I've found that the Frenemy is most cunning when a person decides to make a change in their life. They say that humans are creatures of habit, and new habits are not easy to form. In fact, starting a new habit/routine is one of the hardest things for the brain to accept. Think of it like an elderly person who doesn't want to deal with new technology; NO CHANGE PLEASE!

So don't be surprised if you find CBT exercises, mindfulness or exercise difficult at first. This is completely normal. The rule of thumb is that it takes 21 days to form a new habit, right? But nobody ever explains the reason behind this! Over time I've broken it down to three areas of brain sabotage:

1. Aggressive brain.

2. Sneaky brain.

3. Positive brain.

Stage 1: Aggressive brain

If you're lucky, day one and two of your new routine will go without a hitch. You'll be filled with positive energy and enthusiasm. But suddenly on day three it hits you...

✖ *Thoughts:* You stupid bitch, why did you think this was a good idea? You can't possibly maintain this. You should just give up now.

✖ *Emotions:* Distressed, angry and frustrated.

✖ *Physical:* Overly tired, achy and sluggish.

This is your brain furiously rejecting your new routine, because it's a change to the norm. It usually lasts at least five days. So hang in there!

Stage 2: Sneaky brain

By now it's week two and the aggressive symptoms have started to die down. But then something else starts to emerge...

✖ *Thoughts:* You didn't sleep so well last night, why don't you take today off?

✖ *Emotions:* Indifference and self-pity.

✖ *Physical:* Lethargic and uninterested.

Don't be fooled, it's a trick! The Frenemy is trying to sabotage everything with a new and kinder tactic. Keep going with your routine.

Stage 3: Positive brain

Now it's the final week. You're so close! Suddenly the brain becomes encouraging.

- ✖ *Thoughts:* You've done so well, you should feel really proud. Why not treat yourself to a lie in as a reward?

- ✖ *Emotions:* Satisfied, appeased and happy.

- ✖ *Physical:* Relaxed.

This is the part that normally gets me. But once again it's a trick! This is the Frenemy in her purest form. You've reached the final hurdle, so don't stop now. This is your brain's last-ditch attempt to essentially kill the routine with kindness.

After week three your new habit will become much easier – almost like second nature. It's a hard slog, but if I can do it (and I'm a lazy cow), then believe me, you all have a chance.

TIPS: I have listed my top tips for dealing with the three areas of sabotage with the gym in mind, so adapt them to your situation.

✘ *Be strict.* Normally in life there is room for compromise, but when starting a new routine sticking to the plan 100 per cent is vital. When the alarm clock goes off, DON'T give yourself a moment to think. Just get the f**k up. Or if you do your routine after work, just go – no thinking!

✘ *Incentives:* Nothing works better on me than a bribe. For example, I'll make blueberry pancakes for breakfast before I go out (they only take ten minutes) and eat them whilst watching trashy TV.

✘ *Future thinking:* Try to think about how you want to feel later rather than how you feel now. There's nothing worse than being disappointed with yourself – it's so demoralising. So when the negative thoughts start, just think, 'I know I'll feel proud of myself if I do it.'

✘ *Rewards:* When you've completed a session, reward yourself. I normally have a Starbucks coffee. Positive reinforcement is a great thing.

REMEMBER: IF YOU DO NOTHING, THEN NOTHING WILL CHANGE. Anything, no matter how big or small, is good as long as it involves action. For example, it could be any of the following:

- ✖ Go to see the doctor to discuss your anxiety.

- ✖ Book a session with a CBT therapist (see Chapter 2).

- ✖ Give up coffee or alcohol.

- ✖ Go to that event, even if makes you feel anxious. Come up with a plan if you need to, such as 'I only have to stay for an hour.'

- ✖ Go to a book club regularly.

- ✖ Attend more drinks after work.

Beware the Frenemy! I've curled up with her so many times (and still do on occasion), but she never makes things better. It's similar to constantly putting off a dentist's appointment – it might feel safer to stay at home, but you're only giving the tooth more time to rot.

Chapter 7

ADVICE FOR CAREGIVERS

A few years ago after a particularly rough night, my mum looked at me with tears in her eyes and said, 'I feel powerless because I don't know how to help you. I want to make everything better, but I'm just making it worse.' Despite not having any children of my own, I can imagine how horrible it must be to watch someone you love in pain and not know what to do. If the roles were reversed I know I'd be desperate to help. Despite their best efforts, nothing my parents tried really improved the situation. They didn't know what they were dealing with and I was clueless about how to instruct them. My boyfriend also faced the same dilemma and he certainly bore the brunt of my rage when he said the 'wrong' thing. This in turn made me feel guilty because I knew that he was only trying to help. It was an exhausting cycle.

Here's an example of a typical anxiety-fuelled scenario from my past:

Me:　　　*Crying hysterically* I can't breathe, Mum. Everything is too much. I don't want to go to this party. I'll make a fool of myself.

Mum:　　What do you mean, sweetheart? You'll be fine. Try to calm down.

Me:　　　It's me, I'm a freak! Everyone knows it. I'm going to be miserable for the rest of my life. I can't make it stop.

Mum:　　What? Claire, calm down. You need to calm down. Oh God, I'm making it worse, aren't I?

The above situation is what I refer to as 'a meltdown'. It happens when all of the anxiety that a person has been trying to suppress literally explodes from their mind. I compare it to a river bursting its banks – one that will not stop until all the water has drained (which, in turn, leaves the person feeling drained and depleted of energy). It can be very distressing to watch.

Here's another example:

Me:　　　Oh God, I don't want to go to this dinner tonight. I won't be able to think of anything interesting to say. Your friends will think I'm boring.

Dan: What are you talking about? You're being
             ridiculous!

Me: I'm not being ridiculous. You think I'm a
             freak don't you? Why can't you understand?

Dan: I'm trying, babe, but you're not making
             any sense. Nobody will be scrutinising
             you – they're all nice people. Why do you
             think they'll be focusing on you when
             they have their own lives?

In order to help someone with anxiety, I think it's
essential to understand the problem as a whole and how
it makes them think and feel. One of the biggest problems
concerning mental illness is the lack of guidance.
Unlike a physical condition, such as a stomach bug or
a broken bone, there aren't any clear instructions to
guarantee recovery. Doctors can only make 'suggestions'
without concrete proof. Not exactly the kind of thing
you want to hear when you're desperate (trust me). So
the responsibility for care mainly falls on a person's
nearest and dearest, which can be daunting.

It's also frustrating when your loved ones say
the wrong thing time and again because they don't
understand. This is then accompanied by a wave of
guilt, because you know they're only trying to help.
The end result is that nothing is resolved and you're
doomed to repeat the same patterns in the future.

When I was recovering, I started to think about
the situation in a different way. Only *I* knew what I

needed to hear. So how could I expect my loved ones to help me without telling them how? Would you expect someone to be able to put a flat pack wardrobe together without any instructions? (Not that I ever read them.) If I wanted things to improve, I needed to take a more proactive approach.

I'd like to share some tips from my own personal set of 'instructions' in the hope that they will help others. The first thing to highlight is that anxiety is not a *rational* disorder, so you can't expect the normal things said to comfort a person in distress to be much use. Don't try to treat an irrational problem with rational responses – if anything, it will only make the situation worse.

In my experience, people with anxiety are constantly on the look-out for signs that they are 'not normal'. We're trained detectors of human emotion (because ours are so fine-tuned). If you know someone with anxiety, chances are that they'll have said something similar to this at some point: 'He thinks I'm weird. I could just see it in his eyes, it was obvious.' Or 'I'm sorry, Mum, you must be so fed up with me being like this.' It's a mixture of fear and guilt. Personally, I was afraid of what I call 'the look'. It's difficult to articulate... the 'I don't know what to say' look. It used to fill me with a sense of dread and hopelessness. In a nutshell, it was a gaze that said, 'You're alone and nobody can help you.' There's nothing worse than feeling alone when you're not well. It's a look that I've seen in many people's eyes over the years and although they'd deny this, it doesn't change how it made me feel. (Yes I'm aware that I'm starting to sound paranoid at this point, but read on!)

This isn't a criticism of my parents or friends in any way – I cannot count the ways in which they have tried to help. To be honest, I think that what I construed to be a look of abandonment was most likely fear...they didn't know what to do, and I could see it. Consequently, like many sufferers I began to hide my anxiety. I hid it from my boyfriend, friends and my parents because I couldn't bear to see that look in their eyes and the guilt I felt for causing them so much pain. It was easier to just pretend that everything was OK.

HOW TO HELP SOMEONE WITH ANXIETY

1. Appear 100 per cent calm and confident

I cannot stress this first point enough. Even if you're shitting yourself, do an Oscar-worthy performance and appear the opposite. This is very important because the person having the attack will feed off your emotions and react accordingly. If you're calm, it will help to calm them. If you appear confident that everything will be OK, it will reassure them.

2. Let the attack happen

Don't tell the person to 'stop it' or shout at them to 'calm down!' The attack is already happening and needs to run its course, so don't encourage them to fight it. Also, do not be an overbearing presence and force them to 'get over the attack faster'. Just remain a constant and solid figure who will wait patiently until everything calms down a little (because ultimately it will). Attacks dissipate a lot faster when they are accepted by the brain.

3. Use distraction

No, I don't mean start juggling knives or doing cartwheels around the room! Do something to take the person's mind off the situation. In particular, try something that forces them to engage their brain. Nothing too intense like 'What's 63 x 27?' Perhaps a simple game such as 'How many boys' names can you think of beginning with the letter A?' Distracting the brain is an excellent strategy and if the person experiencing the attacks sees you getting involved then they will be more likely to join in.

Humour is also a very powerful tool. In my experience, laughter neutralises anxiety in the same way that water kills fire – so try to have a joke about the situation. For example, 'Bloody hell you've got steam coming out of your ears, you're like a kettle!'

4. Help with recovery

The advice for an anxiety attack and a panic attack differs slightly here.

Anxiety

After an anxiety attack the person will most likely feel exhausted as it will have burned through their adrenalin and emotional resources. Therefore, help them to feel more comfortable. If you're at home, put them on the couch with a few cushions. Offer to make them their favourite drink (hot chocolate does wonders BTW) and show them affection (hugs, etc.).

If you're in a public place, make them as comfortable as you can (e.g. find a coffee shop or go and sit in the car for 10 minutes). Just find a place in which they feel safe and let them decompress. At this stage *do not* bombard them with questions about why they think the attack happened. Just make small talk and distract them with something (e.g. the TV or music).

Panic

After a panic attack the individual's body will be coursing with adrenalin and this needs to be expended (basically, it needs to get used up as this will reduce the pounding heart symptom). If possible, encourage them to do some exercise and do it with them. One night when I had a horrendous panic attack, my dad took me for a brisk walk in the cold January air. He didn't realise it at the time (as everything was still trial and error) but it was the most helpful thing he ever suggested! It was 10pm, but that didn't bother him. We put on our coats and walked around the streets for ten minutes.

If you can't get outside to exercise, perhaps run up and down the stairs, do some star jumps or have a dance around. It might feel ridiculous but it really helps. (Do not suggest exercise if advised against this by a doctor.)

After the adrenalin has burned off, the person will feel exhausted (physically and mentally), so as above, make them feel comfortable. After our walk, my dad and I sat on the couch together and watched *Catch Me if You Can*. We had a glass of wine and he wrapped his arms around me. I know that might sound quite strange...a 26-year-old woman cuddling her dad on the couch like a child! However, it really helped and provided immense comfort. I felt 100 per cent safe for the first time in ages. You'd be surprised how much the traditional and primitive techniques work.

Again, don't bombard the person with questions at this stage – just let them decompress.

5. Ask if they want to talk

Finally, when everything has calmed down (leave it at least a few hours), ask the person if they want to talk about it. To be honest, a therapist is more likely to be helpful here as they will already fully understand what the person is going through. CBT techniques can be very useful for anxiety (see Chapter 2). I would suggest going through a mental health charity for a recommendation, as NHS waiting lists tend to be lengthy.

Useful phrases to help comfort someone who is having an attack are:

✖ 'Remember this is just a nasty trick. You feel distressed but nothing bad will happen. It's OK.'

✖ 'I'm right here. I'm not going anywhere. We'll work through this together. This is a treatable condition. I'm not giving up on you.'

✖ 'One step at a time, OK? I know you're itching to think ahead and that your mind is buzzing, but we need to try and stay in the present.'

✖ 'You're not the only one. This condition is more common than you think! There's no need to feel embarrassed or ashamed.'

✖ 'Why don't we play a game? There's nothing decent on TV anyway! How about a game of Top Trumps?'

✖ 'Later, when you're feeling calmer, we'll talk about what's troubling you. We'll write them down and go through them together.'

The five DON'Ts

Caregivers make a lot of common mistakes (through no fault of their own) and I'd like to point out the top five:

1. Don't ask questions

From experience, I can barely remember my address when I'm having an anxiety or panic attack. It's almost impossible to think straight. Therefore, asking me multiple questions will provoke an emotional reaction. Even innocent ones such as 'What's wrong?' or 'Why are you shaking?' can frustrate me. When the mind isn't functioning rationally, asking questions will highlight this to the sufferer, thereby making them feel even more stressed. So try to refrain from this completely.

Also, don't try to 'fix' the problem. Men are more guilty of this one to be honest (sorry to play the sexist card). This is probably because they don't menstruate and have therefore never burst into tears over a spilt cup of tea. You cannot fix an anxiety/panic attack, because technically there isn't anything wrong and suggestions will only make matters worse. Just let the sufferer 'feel' their situation without interruption. For example, if they are crying, let them cry. It will release the pressure faster.

2. Don't panic

During a 'freak-out' I'm hypersensitive to the reactions of those around me. Two years ago, during an attack a colleague said to me, 'Oh my God, you're shaking like crazy. Should we call an ambulance? I think we need to call an ambulance immediately!' I won't go into too much detail, but my response was something like, 'F*******ck! Oh my God, is it that bad? Am I dying? Am I going to lose my mind and end up sectioned?'

As a caregiver, this is a tricky mistake to avoid. It's natural to feel distressed if someone you love is in pain. However, it's crucial to try to remain calm. Try to remember that it's an attack – nothing bad will happen physically. (I say this because many sufferers falsely believe they're having a heart attack.) You don't need to worry – it will pass in time. Here are a few things that people have said to me that exposed their own panic: 'Oh God, I don't know what to say,' 'I'm not helping am I?', 'This is really bad' and 'Why can't you calm down?' If in doubt, say very little and simply hold the person close to you. Never underestimate the value of a strong hug!

3. Don't lose your temper

The English are suckers for 'tough love'. We take great pride in the stiff upper lip mentality and this has been passed down through the generations. In many ways this attitude is useful. If in a war-like situation, I'd want to be with a general who kicked arse rather than offered group hugs. However, I can assure you that this is not the approach to take when dealing with an anxious person! Phrases such as 'Pull yourself together,' 'Snap out of it' and 'Stop being soft' will only make things worse. You have to understand that the sufferer is desperate to 'snap out of it', but they don't know how. Kindness and patience are always the better options. Some of the best things to say are simple: 'I love you' and 'I know that you're scared but this will pass.'

It's also important to note that anxiety sufferers constantly worry that they are a 'burden' to their caregivers and will apologise frequently. I do this all the time and it drives my boyfriend mad. So be prepared to repeat reassurances A LOT. Pretend that you're talking to a robot that forgets everything after ten minutes. It's difficult, I'm sure, but stay calm and don't lose your temper.

4. Don't force them to 'think positive'

This one is difficult to explain, so bear with me. Imagine that someone close to you has just died and you're naturally very sad. Now imagine that a friend says 'Look on the bright side' or 'Think about positive things.' How useless and infuriating would that piece of advice be? OK, now apply this scenario to an anxiety sufferer, because that's how they feel when you say the same thing to them. Not that I'm in any way suggesting the pain of loss felt after a bereavement is the same as an anxiety attack, but the feeling of hopelessness is similar. YOU CANNOT THINK POSITIVELY BECAUSE...
a) you can barely think straight, let alone positively;
b) The brain is flooded with negative emotions and any attempt to battle them is fruitless. It's best to let these feelings dissipate naturally.

In a nutshell, pointing out the person's inability to think 'happy thoughts' during an attack is about as much use as a chocolate teapot.

5. Don't stop them from doing what feels right

This one is subjective, so don't take it as gospel – for example, if your loved one feels that slicing his/her fingers off 'feels right', I would recommend an intervention!

However, it's important to remember that the brain is a remarkable thing and will eventually adapt to comfort itself. Therefore, don't try to prevent this from happening. During a panic attack I like to:

- ✖ sit on the floor in the hallway – it's weird I know, but I find it soothing

- ✖ have Dan either sat next to me or stood in the kitchen where I can see him – Rigby my dog usually sits at my feet

- ✖ repeat the phrase 'I'm so scared' at least five times

- ✖ drink a small glass of red wine whilst reading a book out loud – again it's weird, but it helps.

Dan barely registers any of the above these days. It's completely 'normal' in our flat! He'd admit that during my first attacks he would try to make me sit on the couch or drink some water. But he now listens and trusts my instincts, which is the best thing.

So my point is, if a loved one wants to do something 'slightly unconventional', then let them, whether that be crying in the bath, lying on the kitchen floor or singing nursery rhymes. However, as I said, this one is also subjective. So play it by ear. For instance, I wouldn't let someone run around the house screaming, as this is erratic and unhelpful behaviour. But rather than stopping them point blank, perhaps suggest that you go for a walk to burn off the adrenalin.

Comfort is a precious thing to someone who is suffering with mental illness. The presence of a friendly face and calming words can do wonders.

CHARITIES AND USEFUL ORGANISATIONS

Finally, I recommend that you have a look on the leading mental health websites as these offer lots of general advice and tips for caregivers.

United Kingdom
Anxiety UK
www.anxietyuk.org.uk

Anxiety UK is a national registered charity formed in 1970, by someone living with agoraphobia, for those affected by anxiety, stress and anxiety based depression.

'The Caregiver's Guide to Anxiety' is available to buy from www.anxietyuk.org.uk/products/anxiety-condition/children-and-anxiety/the-caregivers-guide-to-anxiety

Mind
www.mind.org.uk

Mind is a mental health charity that provides advice and support to empower anyone experiencing a mental health problem and campaigns to improve services, raise awareness and promote understanding.

'How to cope as a carer' is available to download from www.mind.org.uk/information-support/helpingsomeone-else/carers-friends-and-family-a-guide-tocoping/#.VubuxPmLTIU

United States and Canada

Anxiety and Depression Association of America
www.adaa.org

ADAA is an international non-profit organisation dedicated to the prevention, treatment, and cure of anxiety, depressive, obsessive-compulsive and trauma-related disorders through education, practice and research.

Anxiety Disorders Association of Canada
www.anxietycanada.ca

ADAC is a registered Canadian non-profit organisation whose aim is to promote the prevention, treatment and management of anxiety disorders and to improve the lives of people who suffer from them.

Australia and New Zealand

Beyond Blue

www.beyondblue.org.au

Beyond Blue provides information and support to help everyone in Australia achieve their best possible mental health, whatever their age and wherever they live.

Mental Health Foundation of New Zealand

www.mentalhealth.org.nz

The Mental Health Foundation of New Zealand is a charity that works towards creating a society free from discrimination, where all people enjoy positive mental health and wellbeing.

'Worried about someone' is available at www.mentalhealth.org.nz/get-help/in-crisis/worried-about-someone

Chapter 8

TAKE ACTION!

I hope that by this point you'll have a better grasp on what social anxiety is and will have identified which areas are applicable to you. So what next? Well, now you need to establish a recovery plan! A large proportion of people are procrastinators. For example, 'Oh my God, that is such a great idea! I'll start looking into it tomorrow.' Four weeks later and they still haven't done anything. My advice is to start your recovery plan first thing tomorrow morning before you do anything else and before the brain is bombarded with other things.

MAKING A PLAN

There's no 'one size fits all' when it comes to mental health. Everything can and should be personalised. A plan is a good idea, as it will keep you on track. Studies suggest that people are more likely to achieve their goals if they have a strategy. My advice is to designate at least one hour for drafting your plan and break it down into sections, complete with dates. Be realistic with time frames.

Doctor's appointment

✖ Book an appointment NOW before you bottle it. If you feel as though you might be nervous or emotional and need extra time, book a double appointment.

✖ Write a list of your physical and emotional symptoms to help you to be concise.

✖ Discuss the various medication options with your doctor.

Medication plan

✖ Pick a weekend to start taking your medication (if you choose to go down this route). There's no guarantee that you'll experience side effects, but it's better to be prepared.

✖ Tell family/friends so that they can be aware/ prepared if you want to hibernate for a few days.

✖ Have lots of goodies ready to get you through the weekend. Think of it as a good thing. How many times in life do you have the perfect excuse to do nothing?!

Therapy

✖ Think about what therapy most appeals to you and do some research online. Talk to a call handler at Mind or Anxiety UK if you would like some expert advice.

✖ In my opinion, it's worth doing some element of exposure therapy (see Chapter 2) once you feel comfortable, as this is very effective for social anxiety. It will also help to build your confidence.

Exercise

✖ Slowly incorporate some kind of exercise into your weekly routine. I'm sure you can find a spare 30 minutes at least twice a week.

✖ Book it in your diary like an actual appointment. It cannot be cancelled or overlooked.

✖ Create a playlist to keep yourself motivated while you exercise.

Down time

✖ Again, as with exercise, schedule in at least two hours of down time a week. I usually have an hour on Tuesday evenings and Sunday afternoons.

✖ Warn people in advance so that you're not disturbed, and turn off your phone.

✖ Down time can be anything from reading, watching a TV show or having a bath. The point is to have some time to yourself in order to recharge.

Diet

✖ Slowly cut down on caffeine and alcohol. In my opinion cold turkey isn't a good idea as it's too extreme. Instead, lower your amount each day.

✖ Start incorporating salmon and spinach into your diet (refer back to pages 53-56).

✖   ✖   ✖

It might seem a bit overwhelming at first, but in time it will simply become routine. You don't have to do everything at once! Designate a month as your deadline to get everything in order. Think about how much time you spend watching TV or browsing the internet. I'm sure you can find the time to help yourself heal

RELAPSE

I don't like to use the word 'relapse' because it implies addiction. However, slipping back into bad habits does happen. Even with all my experience I still sometimes fall off the wagon and forget to take care of myself. But that's OK. It's unrealistic to presume that once you conquer your anxiety you'll never hear from it again. To repeat a physical analogy, would you be devastated if you got more than one cold in your lifetime? Of course not – it happens, and in time you will heal. Try to apply this to mental health. The same techniques will work again and it'll most likely be easier the second time round. Relapse isn't a failure – it's just part of life and there's nothing to be ashamed of.

The first aid kit that I mentioned in Chapter 2 is very useful in this scenario. It's there to support you when you need a little extra help. Feel bad for a while and when you're ready get back into the routine that helped last time.

You CAN do this – believe in your own strength. A good friend once told me, 'There aren't many people in life who'll be in your corner, so you better bloody had be.'

Chapter 9

AND FINALLY...

As I write this, I'm two weeks away from getting married. That's right - I'll be a married woman by the time this book is published, although I still don't feel old enough to be a Mrs and I point blank refuse to become an adult!

Now it's strange to think of that terrible time three years ago. The girl who was convinced that her life was over and that she would lose everything seems like a stranger. Time and a good dose of inner acceptance helped her to regain faith in both herself and the world.

I didn't have a makeover or spend a year travelling in order to 'find myself'. I worked hard to tackle my mental health issues and I'm proud of how far I've come.

I send my love and support to all those affected by social anxiety and panic attacks. Don't give up. Take one step at a time. The hard times will pass...because they always do.

GLOSSARY OF MADNESS

To finish off, here is a random cluster of information that you might find useful.

BOOKS

Barrett, Grace, Devon, Natasha and Mendoza, Nadia (2015) *The Self-Esteem Team's Guide to Sex, Drugs and WTFs?!!* London: John Blake Publishing.

Cain, Susan (2013) *Quiet: The Power of Introverts in a World That Can't Stop Talking.* London: Penguin.

Carbonell, David (2004) *Panic Attacks Workbook.* Berkeley, CA: Ulysses Press.

Haig, Matt (2015) *Reasons to Stay Alive.* Edinburgh: Canongate Books.

Hughes, Neil (2015) *Walking on Custard & the Meaning of Life: A Guide for Anxious Humans.* UK: Enthusiastic Whim.

Powell, Trevor (2009) *The Mental Health Handbook: A Cognitive Behavioural Approach* (3rd edition). London: Speechmark Publishing.

APPS

Headspace
Mindpilot

WEBSITES

Anxiety Slayer
www.anxietyslayer.com

Childline
www.childline.org.uk

HeadMeds
www.headmeds.org.uk

Student Minds
www.studentminds.org.uk

The Adrenal Fatigue Solution
https://adrenalfatiguesolution.com

YoungMinds
www.youngminds.org.uk

BLOGS/VLOGS

https://weallmadhere.com – MINE, obviously ;)

Ruby Ray: *www.youtube.com/channel/UCvM9-5wnW45mqPsXlMYwglQ*

Laura Lejeune: *www.youtube.com/channel/UC99LFxQRYI0d-SeXAzDpCrQ*

LikeKristen: *www.youtube.com/channel/UCqbNeeBXyD21OzwRySul5gw*

Laura Nuttall: *www.youtube.com/channel/UCA5ugRUbYWzSl1opVCZ5k-A*

Diary of a Social Phobic: *https://diaryofasocialphobic.wordpress.com*

The Social Phobic: *https://socialphobic.co.uk*

The Seeds 4 Life: *www.theseeds4life.com*

PEOPLE TO FOLLOW ON TWITTER

Matt Haig
Natasha Devon
@rachelgriffin22
@asklikekristen
@_SelfEsteemTeam
@PookyH
@bryony_gordon

CHARITIES AND ORGANISATIONS

UK
Anxiety UK
www.anxietyuk.org.uk

Mind
www.mind.org.uk

Time to Change
www.time-to-change.org.uk

The Samaritans
www.samaritans.org

US and Canada
Anxiety and Depression Association of Canada
www.adaa.org

Anxiety Disorders Association of Canada
www.anxietycanada.ca

Australia and New Zealand
Beyond Blue
www.beyondblue.org.au

Mental Health Foundation of New Zealand
www.mentalhealth.org.nz

REFERENCES

Adams, R. (2015, 14 May) 'Surge in young people seeking help for exam stress.' *The Guardian*. Available at www.theguardian.com/education/2015/may/14/calls-to-childline-over-exam-stress-break-records, accessed on 30 July 2016.

Anxiety UK (2015) Available at https://www.anxietyuk.org.uk/about-us, accessed on 30 July 2016.

Devon, N. (2015) Personal interview. Available at http://weallmadhere.com/2015/12/17/the-devon-effect, accessed on 30 July 2016.

Hochman, D. (2014, 19 September) 'Amy Cuddy takes a stand.' *New York Times*. Available at www.nytimes.com/2014/09/21/fashion/amy-cuddy-takes-a-stand-TED-talk.html?_r=2, accessed on 30 July 2016.

MacLean, P. D. (1990) *The Triune Brain in Evolution: Role in Paleocerebral Functions*. New York, NY: Springer.

Rohn, J. (2014, 18 September) Available at www.facebook.com/OfficialJimRohn/posts/10154545246315635, accessed on 30 July 2016.